Books by the Author

My Journey to Peace with PTSD (on Kindle)
Apitherapy – From a Beekeeper's Perspective
BEe Perspective Beekeeping

BEe Perspective Beekeeping

by
Lady Spirit Moon Cerelli
Former Ambassador for the Center for Honeybee Research

BEe Perspective Beekeeping

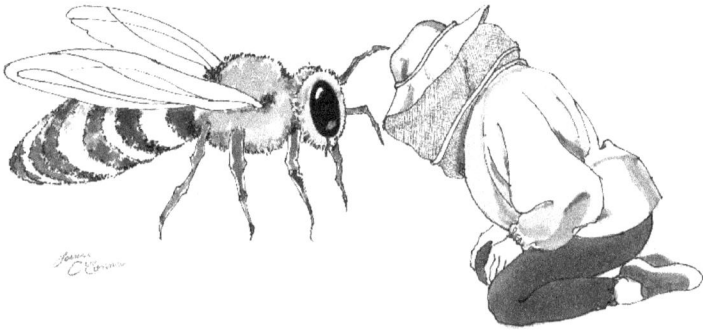

by
Lady Spirit Moon Cerelli
Former Ambassador, Center for Honeybee Research
Certified Beekeeper
Certified Apitherapist
Master Herbalist
Certified Nutritionist

Foreword by Les Crowder
Author of *Top-Bar Beekeeping*

BEe Perspective Beekeeping

ISBN-13: 978-0-9798883-4-2

Library of Congress Registration Number TXu 2-117-143

Version 1:1

First Printing, January, 2019 (paperback edition, 9" x 6")

Author: Lady Spirit Moon Cerelli

Acknowledgments

I would like to take this opportunity to thank the many scientists of the world who did their research to afford me and you the opportunity to better understand what a wondrous creature the honeybee is.

This includes:

- Dr. Don Huber, Emeritus Professor, Purdue University, my personal friend and science mentor

- Les Crowder

- Michael Bush for his detailed edit suggestions

- Dr. Lee Barnes, PhD in Environmental Horticulture, an experienced naturalist, dedicated environmental activist, and professional dowser

- Dr. Anthony Samsel, independent scientist and researcher

- Dr. Stephanie Seneff, biologist and researcher, MIT

- Dr. Tom Seely, Horace White Professor, Biology, Department of Neurobiology and Behavior, Cornell University (Dr. Seely provided permission to reprint his *Suggested Darwinian Beekeeping* in this book)

- All other scientists, farmers, and beekeepers here and around the world from whom I sought advice and shared information with me

- All my students from the past, present, and future for allowing me to teach them Mother Earth's way of keeping her girls

This book is dedicated to the honeybees for their knowledge and sacrifices for pollinating our food and offering their hive products and life for our health. I also dedicate this book to all treatment-free beekeepers who stand in the face of criticism because they chose a safe method of keeping our bees safe when others choose not to see or hear our sisters.

About the Author

Founder & President, BEe Healing Guild
Former Ambassador, Center for
Honeybee Research, 2010
Certified Beekeeper, 2008
Certified Apitherapist, 2012
Master Herbalist, 2011
Certified Nutritionist, 2010

Lady Spirit Moon Cerelli owns and operates BEe Healing Apiary in the Spring Creek Community of Hot Springs, North Carolina, and is the founder of the non-profit BEe Healing Guild, Org. Since 2008, she has raised resistant bees using the BEe Perspective's treatment-free methods.

In 1984, Lady received her certification in herbology and did clinical work while owning the largest herb farm in Michigan's northern part of the Lower Peninsula. She taught 63 workshops consisting of herbal medicine, live wreath-making, basket weaving, potpourri, and creating perfume. Lady is a fiber artist and her weavings are on display across the United States and in the Virgin Islands.

She moved to northwestern North Carolina in 2005 to the Appalachian Mountains where she now resides. Through the years, Lady found a love for wholesome living including nutrition and herbs. It was in the spring of 2008 that she found a passion for beekeeping. This passion and her knowledge in herbology led her to design, wholesale, and retail her own body lotion from products of the beehive, exotic oils, and herbal tinctures. This formula has been given to another who is doing well in retailing it.

Lady has also sponsored a project in Senegal, Africa. She continues to educate through email, Facebook, Skype, and classrooms. Since her first visit to Africa, Lady and her Senegalese family have adopted each other and become a surrogate family. There is now a Little Lady about four years old.

Lady writes for bee magazines and newsletters – including the blogs and newsletters for the BEe Healing Guild. Her recent book, *Apitherapy: From a BEekeeper's Perspective*, is also available here at the Guild's website store. The book contains information on all hive products, how to sustainably harvest the products, as well as a special section on bee venom and stinging for Lyme disease. Pictures are also included in the book to show how products should look.

In 2010, she was appointed Ambassador for the Center for Honeybee Research in Asheville, North Carolina. That same October, she traveled to Turin, Italy, as a Slow Food Delegate and met with professionals and beekeepers while attending the Terre Madre's International Slow Food Festival. In 2011, she traveled back over the pond to Italy for a 17-day, 3-city tour to meet with more professionals and beekeepers from Turin down to Bologna, and others who have created Italy's largest beekeeping cooperative. Lady spent the final five days in Toulouse, France, where she stayed with Dr. John Kefuss, known worldwide for raising resistant queens. Dr. Kefuss speaks many languages and teaches globally on how to artificially inseminate honeybee queens.

Lady still maintains her global contacts of beekeepers and scientists.

Foreword

Lady Spirit Moon called me a few years ago to invite me to a gathering of beekeepers in North Carolina. I didn't know her, had just undergone some difficult transitions and surgery, just moved, and was trying to settle my family in Texas. But something in her voice and attitude made me feel like I should try to get to that gathering. It turned out to be a gathering of people looking for a better way to work with bees. It was a much-needed meetup of far flung people that needed to inspire each other. It was a meeting in which Lady said often "Listen to the bees." That simple sentence gives us a compass to navigate our path forward.

Our culture has been one of fighting the dangerous parts of nature and each other for survival. Our old culture would make us look at bees as livestock in our control. We wanted as much honey as we could get. We tried to control the biology of the beehive with only our honey production in mind. We are now witnessing a shift in attitude. Rather than fight the dangerous parts of nature (predators, pests, and parasites of ourselves or our crops, each other) are beginning to realize the need to learn to work with nature. We are not competing with nature; we are part of it. We are biological creatures tied to and nourished by nature. We cannot live without our fellow creatures. Lady's respect for nature, and the nature of honeybees, guides her and any who can listen to a relationship with honeybees. That allows bees to live more as they would live on their own. We have interacted with bees by insisting that they comply with our imperfect understanding of how we think they should live with our desire for honey production or most recently mobile pollination. Her use of probiotics to prevent brood disease in honeybees is a beautiful example of working with nature and our fellow organisms to enhance health, rather than fight the "bad" parts of nature with poisons. We have tried poisons for the last four to seven decades. It turns out they accumulate and poison our bees, ourselves, and everything else. We are proving that poisons are toxic.

Lady's lessons in beekeeping are about health and detoxification. We now realize that the ocean, the air, the soil, our bees, and we are in need of detoxification. Just as the ocean does not need yet more plastic or mercury, our bees do not need more toxic inputs and disruptions to their natural biology. This book is a call to drop the pretense that we know what cell size is best, how many drones they should be allowed to have and let them decide for themselves. When we listen to them, we enter into a relationship where what they need or even want is considered. It makes beekeepers cooperators with bees rather than dictators of the bee's lives. It can take years to get good at "listening" to the bees, but Lady's call to listen will alert you to the need to start out with some respect for their natural and beautiful biology.

There are things Lady does that I don't. I prefer topbar hives that do not require frames or foundation, and she has inspired me to try probiotics. I live with Africanized bees and have gotten to like them. Calendar dates, seasons, and flowers are always dependent on where you are. She keeps bees in the mountains of North Carolina, and you the reader are wherever you are. I go between nearly tropical Austin, Texas, and the tropical island of Jamaica, so the dates have to be adjusted to the flowers and climate. But her call to shift our perspective is exactly what many people are beginning to realize is needed today. The only way we are going to rise is if we all rise together. If we step on bees to get "ahead," we will fall with them. They are fellow creatures that we need in this amazing journey. If there are generations in the future, they will look back on this time as the time when we began to use our intelligence and our wisdom to work with nature rather than against it. This is when we began to listen to the bees. If we don't begin to listen to nature, we will fall with the birds and the bees and the flowers and the trees till we're up to our knees in cancer, dementia, diabetes, and any survivors will say "we should have listened to the bees." It is time to all rise together!

Les Crowder is the coauthor of *Top-Bar Beekeeping*. He has devoted his entire adult life to the study and care of honeybees. Dedicated to finding organic and natural solutions for problems commonly treated with chemicals, he designed his own top-bar hives and set about discovering how to treat disease and genetic weaknesses through plant medicine and selective breeding. He has been a leader in his community, having served as New Mexico's honeybee inspector and president of the New Mexico Beekeepers Association. He is an avid storyteller and has spoken annually at the New Mexico Organic Farm Conference for over 15 years. Les is also a certified teacher and enjoys teaching children Spanish and science. Les has three wonderful children: Emily, Peter, and Ben. He is currently married to Heather Harrell, and they work their bees and certified organic/biodynamic farm together, where they raise sheep and poultry as well as honeybees.

Table of Contents

About the Author i

Foreword... iii

Table of Contents vii

Introduction – Why BEe Perspective........................... 1

Darwinion Beekeeping... 9

2: Why BEe Perspective 25

    Treating with Chemicals...................................26

    Combining Hives 27

    Weakening the Gene Pool 28

    Using Diseased Equipment 29

    Failing to Feed Properly 29

    Pollinating Crops 30

    Feral Bees 31

3: Bee Equipment You'll Need 33

    Beehive Bodies 35

    Beekeeping Tools 37

    Beehive Bodies and Frames............................39

        4.9 mm Foundation...................................*40*

        Housel Position for Foundation *41*

        Plastic Frames *43*

        Old Frames *45*

        Color Codes *45*

4: A New Home for Your Bees 47

    Locating Your Apiary 47

    Using Geomagnetic Lines 48

    Placing Your Hives...57

5: Nuc/Package Care 61

Installing Packaged Bees 61

Installing Your Nuc of Bees 62

Splitting a Full Hive 64

Observing Your Swarms 66

Raising Queens 67

6: Hive Inspection 69

Approaching Your Hives 69

Inspecting a Langstroth Hive 71

Wear Appropriate Clothing 75

Move Respectively 75

Raise the telescoping lid and smell 75

Get Out When Bees are Excited 76

Go Into the Hive 77

Make the Actual Inspection 78

Inspect Frames 79

Put the Frames Back Together 81

Brood Pattern 82

7: Communicate with Your Bees 85

Learn Different Colony Castes 85

Listen to Your Bees 87

Know About Bee Pheromones 91

Alarm Pheromone 92

Brood Recognition Pheromone 92

Drone Pheromone 93

DuFour's Gland Pheromone 93

Egg Marking Pheromone 93

Footprint Pheromone 93

Forager Pheromone 94

Nasonov Pheromone 94

Other Pheromones *94*

Queen Mandibular Pheromone *94*

Queen Retinue Pheromone *94*

8: Honeybee Diseases and Pests 97

Acarine Disease 98

American Foulbrood (AFB) 98

Chalkbrood Disease 101

Chilled Brood 101

European Foulbrood (EFB) 102

Idiopathic Brood Disease Syndrome (IBDS) 103

Nosema Disease 104

Black Queen Cell Virus (BQCV) 106

Small Hive Beetle 106

Stonebrood Disease 108

Varroa Destructor (Varroa Mite) 108

Chronic Bee Paralysis Virus (CBPV) *110*

Acute Bee Paralysis Virus (ABPV) *111*

Cloudy Wing Virus (CWV) *111*

Deformed Wing Virus (DWV) *111*

Sacbrood Disease *112*

Wax Moths 113

9: Healing Formulas 117

The Importance of pH Levels 119

Two Formulas 123

Method 1: Lacto Water *123*

Lacto Water to Treat EFB 125

Method 2: Honey Formula *126*

10: The Second Year 129

Inspecting Your Hives 129

Your Inspection *129*

Splitting_Your Hive.. 128

Mating Your Queen...133

11: Planting Your Garden.................................. 137

Plants Your Bees Like...137

Chemicals Hazardous to Honeybees............................148

12: Fascinating Facts.................................... 149

The Charged Flower...149

Bees See Heat Patterns in Flowers 150

Who Decides the Caste 150

Bees Can Smell...150

Bee Venom and Hormones 151

Adrenal Cortex Hormones:..151

Adrenal Medulla Hormones.......................................152

Afterword 155

References.. 159

Introduction – Why BEe Perspective

I began beekeeping with the idea of having only a couple of hives for a little honey. Within three years, I had built my apiary up to 24 hives in three apiaries far enough apart for the queens from my splits to mate with drones from different areas. I learned early that diverse genetics make for a healthier colony. Other beekeepers continually pressed me to treat the bees, but I couldn't bring myself to do it. For three years they would ask how my bees were doing and I would respond that they were still alive and healthy. Not only did my beehives survive for years, the only pests I had were the ones that came with the swarms, but they didn't last for very long. Folks stopped asking.

In the spring following my first year of beekeeping, I watched a bee pull another bee out of a dollop of honey. The rescuer then used its tongue (proboscis) to clean the other bee's wing. I picked up the cleaned bee and placed her on a frame. This showed me that honeybees are compassionate, which is one of the three traits of a sentient being. The summer of the same year, during a hard dearth, I had a hard time keeping the wasps out of the hives during inspections and killed all that I could with my thumb or hive tool. At one point, I watched four bees gather in a half circle around a wasp and guide it toward my thumb. When the bees backed up, I crushed the wasp. Intelligence is the second trait of a sentient being.

I know workers kick the drones out of the hive before winter and while it may not be very ceremonial, the bees do deal with their dead which is called the "rite of death ceremony." This is the third trait of a sentient being. Seeing the traits of a sentient being in the honeybee forever changed my view point of beekeeping.

When I was appointed the post of Ambassador for the Center for Honeybee Research, I started recording my hive inspections and kept detailed notes of everything including times, date, weather, etc. I cut back on the number of hives so that I would have more time to go through and scrutinize everything in the hives. My goal was for honeybee survival and not for honey production. The bees taught me about hive personalities; sound communication; odors; when to go into a hive, when to stay out; how to control pests using the earth's geomagnetic lines; and much more. I have learned that the honeybee is very electrical-minded when it comes to working with the earth. The honeybee also tells me what kind of winter we will have. They communicate so much through their sounds, behavior, and how and where they store their food.

In a lot of writings regarding the honeybees, you will see it written as two words. In some writings, it is written as one word. I prefer the one-word spelling because to me it denotes the honeybees' importance in our world of food. It also sets them apart from other pollinators as everything about the honeybee, hive products, bee venom in the stinger, larvae, and the bee itself is healing for all other animals, including human beings. It also shows the collective harmony of the colony and the fact that the colony is a superorganism.

One of the reasons the honeybee is called a superorganism is their ability to regulate hive temperature[i]:

> *"The bees of a colony in their totality perform a series of activities which give the colony the status of a self-contained entity. This entity – seen as an organism of a high order – is regulated by joint activities which can be placed at the same level as the vegetative functions of higher organisms."*

Rudolf Steiner, a bee lecturer in Stuttgart, Germany, from the turn of the twentieth century also talks about hive temperature[ii]:

> *"When you investigate the temperature in a beehive, you find it to be about the same temperature as that of human blood. The whole beehive develops a temperature comparable to that of blood because, in accordance with the nature of its being, it goes back to the same source as does the human blood."*

In his book *The Spiritual Foundations of Beekeeping,* Iwer Thor Lorenzen writes[iii]:

> *"Apis mellifica do not all have one common group-soul, but each colony, at the soul-level, is an individuality in its own right; one could also call it a 'bee personality.' The group-soul – the conscious spirit of the bee colony – lives in super-sensible worlds and can be greeted there in full consciousness by the bee as a sister being...*

> *"This exceptional greatness of the bee spirits – in certain respects are higher than the human soul – is connected with the fact that they did not take into themselves the forces of lower egotism...."*

Believing the honeybees are my spiritual sisters, I have learned to communicate with them. They taught me that they are indeed a superorganism that only wants to be left alone to do their thing, and yet are willing to help us in our healing. Tears come to my eyes when I think of what humans are doing to them regarding *keeping* them and what we are doing to our environment.

I keep honeybees for the purpose of their survival by learning how they live in their environment and how our environment is hurting them in many ways, on many levels. BEe Perspective Beekeeping is more than just not treating. The BE of BEe means you (the human), the Being, are part of their lives, work their hives with them, and honor them the way they wish to be kept. This is done by observing the colony, learning its personality, and especially listening to their sounds.

Humans want so much to be a part of a good thing that it is difficult for them to set aside their egos. This is what needs to be done when using BEe Perspective methods. The bees know what they are doing. Your primary role is providing a space and protection. In turn, they will allow you to watch, experience, share, learn, and participate in their world. They will show you how they are connected to Mother Earth and Her electrical energy. Bees can see heat patterns, feel the static electricity of a flower containing pollen, and when swarming, use geomagnetic lines to prevent pests in the hives.

Honeybees have lived for millions of years and evolved to colonization about 10,000 years ago. They have collected wisdom, developed organizational skills, and mastered a democratic order of such that cannot be matched by any other societies. They don't want you to redo what Mother Nature has engrained into them for millions of years or to reteach them just because it would be more convenient for you.

Honeybees can teach you to:

- have patience
- sense your environment when listening to the wind or to the water running in the creek
- appreciate Mother working with them in relation to the sun
- perceive nectar in a flower through their vision, heat, and electromagnetic fields (EMFs)
- use geomagnetic lines in the earth for pest control
- understand their organizational skills and systems

4

- and much, much more

I walk the "Red Road," meaning I do my best to honor everything and everyone. I take nothing without giving something back, be it a prayer, a touch, a look, a simple thought, or a hug. With such a belief system, I recognize the need for something to die with dignity without dragging out its life just because I want to keep it around or feel sorry for it. I don't believe things simply die and never exist again. Mother taught me how the Universe recycles everything, including life. The body goes back into the soil that nourished it and the soul goes back to the source. I also watch Mother to see how she works and interacts with her children in caring for them and do what I can to copy her efforts. I confess that Mother and my ignorance have often humbled me.

In 2016, the Xerces Society requested that the bumblebee, be placed on the endangered species list due to the 90 percent loss in 2015. The honeybee is not too far behind. Globally, we are losing a great many of our pollinators because of chemicals being used in agriculture; large monocultures; essential oils and chemicals used in the beehives which affect the hive's bacteria; bad beekeeping practices; to name just a few.

Another reason honeybees are dying is due to beekeepers transporting large numbers of hives over several thousand miles to pollinate large monocrops. Honeybees did not evolve to having their hives (homes) moved. Once the destination is reached, the pollinators use their nuclei (nucs) to create more colonies due to the colony deaths that occurred during transportation. The bees then must contend with harvesting one crop. Poly crops are needed for honeybee survival as their diet needs to be as diverse as humans for health purposes. At one time, Africa was a place considered pest- and chemical-free. Now, some of their beekeepers are being taught to use chemicals in the hives and monoculture farmers are using genetically modified organisms (GMO) and no-till farming practices.

Farmers are under the impression they must "feed the world." I feel this is an oxymoron to the saying, "Feed a man a fish and he will eat for a day. Teach a man to fish and he will eat for a lifetime." What we should be doing for optimum pollinator and human health is to teach farmers and individuals how to grow their own food in the same place from which they drink their water. Teach them to keep a couple hives to pollinate their crops and perhaps have enough for a honey crop. As for the farmer, he can hire someone to care for their hundreds of hives.

Our forefathers had the right idea of planting gardens near the village and using nearby water sources. They used their leftover vegetable scraps, animal manure, and products from the nearby woods to feed back to the soil; recycled from nature to give back to nature. If they lived in an environment of seasons that included cold weather, they learned to preserve and store their food. It was food they either grew themselves, killed, or harvested from the wild. Our ancestors were far healthier than people are today because they became good land stewards by working with the land and with the Mother that nourished them. It was a beautiful union where humans ate healthy, non-contaminated food, yet maintained a strong body through labor.

This book contains very detailed information on subjects that I feel are important, including plastic and why it should not be used in beehives. Geomagnetic lines in the earth is another subject I feel is crucial to hive pest management. Working closely with Mother, I learned how She provides knowledge in caring for Her children. We just need to watch and listen. I hope that you can learn how to look at your honeybees as sentient beings and not just as insects. Everything on the earth was made to work together. Even the chaos teaches us what order is.

Mentors can't always be knowledgeable when teaching you about your hives because they are not the ones always going into your beehives. When it comes to education, have all the teachers you want, attend all your club meetings, read all your books, do your research, and ask all your questions. In the end, your bees will communicate to you what they want and if you learn to watch and listen, they will show you a magical world unlike any you could ever imagine.

Lady Spirit Moon
Beekeeper

Special Note: I would like to give special thanks to Michael Bush for his comments, views, and edit suggestions on this book.

1: Darwinian Beekeeping

If you look into a honeybee hive you will see and hear the past, present, and future of the world. Depending on the speaker or author, the Hymenoptera family of insects is somewhere between 50 to 150 million years old. According to H. A. Dade of the International Bee Research Association, "... it is estimated the honeybee *Apis mellifera* came into existence

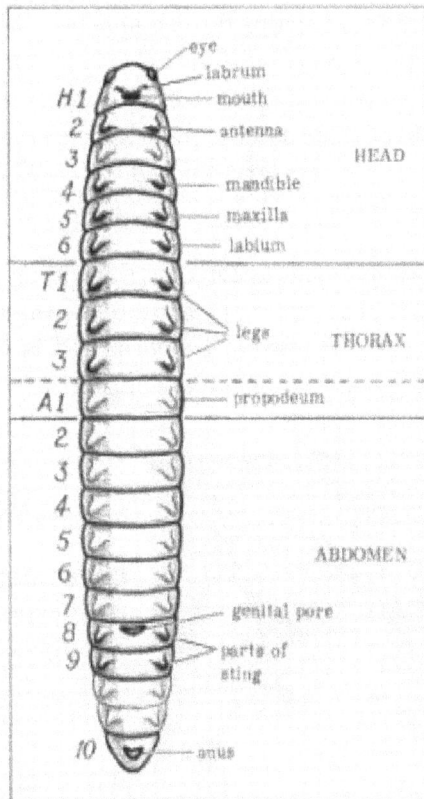

about 10,000 years ago as a worm. As in the above picture, the earliest fossils were in East African gum copal." The honeybee started out as a solitary bee and – in step with the earth's floral kingdom – eventually evolved into a social, superorganism colony.

I was told a long time ago that there is a tonal quality in the sounds made by certain animals that indicate the age of their ancestry. You can hear the honeybee's ancestry in the queens' voices before they emerge from their cells: quacks, honks, sounds of whales, and others.

Of all the pollinators in the world, the honeybee is the most important because it doesn't cross-pollinate flowers. The honeybee maintains the integrity of our food as it moves from flower to flower on the same species of plant. The pollen collected on its hairy body pollinates each flower. When finished with the flower species, the honeybee thoroughly cleans its body, and then goes out and harvests from another plant. Other pollinators like wasps or bumble bees harvest without regard to the plant species (i.e., if an apple is gnarly or dented, it was pollinated by a something other than a honeybee.)

Below are suggestions for Darwinian beekeeping by Thomas D. Seeley, professor of the Department of Neurobiology and Behavior of Cornell University. It is reprinted here with the kind permission from the author:

Seeley, Thomas

Darwinian Beekeeping: An Evolutionary Approach to Apiculture

American Bee Journal, 277-282

Evolution by natural selection is a foundational concept for understanding the biology of honeybees, but it has rarely been used to provide insights into the craft of beekeeping. This is unfortunate because solutions to the problems of beekeeping and bee health may come most rapidly if we are as attuned to the biologist Charles R. Darwin as we are to the Reverend Lorenzo L. Langstroth.

Adopting an evolutionary perspective on beekeeping may lead to better understanding about the maladies of our bees, and ultimately improve our beekeeping and the pleasure we get from our bees. An important first step toward developing a Darwinian perspective on beekeeping is to recognize that honeybees have a stunningly long evolutionary history, evident from the fossil record. One of the most beautiful of all insect fossils is that of a worker honeybee, in the species Apis henshawi, discovered in 30-million-year-old shales from Germany. There also exist superb fossils of our modern honeybee species, Apis mellifera, in amber-like materials collected in East Africa that are about 1.6 million years old (Engel 1998).

We know, therefore, that honeybee colonies have experienced millions of years being shaped by the relentless operation of natural selection. Natural selection maximizes the abilities of living systems (such honeybee colonies) to pass on their genes to future generations. Colonies differ in their genes; therefore, colonies differ in all the traits that have a genetic basis, including colony defensiveness, vigor in foraging, and resistance to diseases. The colonies best endowed with genes favoring colony survival and reproduction in their locale have the highest success in passing their genes on to subsequent generations, so over time the colonies in a region become well adapted to their environment.

This process of adaptation by natural selection produced the differences in worker bee color, morphology, and behavior that distinguish the 27 subspecies of Apis mellifera (e.g., A.m. mellifera, A. m. ligustica, and A. m. scutellata) that live within the species' original range of Europe, western Asia, and Africa (Ruttner 1988). The colonies in each subspecies are precisely adapted to the climate, seasons, flora, predators, and diseases in their region of the world.

Moreover, within the geographical range of each subspecies natural selection produced ecotypes, which are fine-tuned, locally adapted populations. For example, one ecotype of the subspecies Apis mellifera evolved in the Landes region of southwest France, with its biology tightly linked to the massive bloom of heather (Calluna vulgaris L.) in August and September. Colonies native to this region have a second strong peak of brood rearing in August that helps them exploit this heather bloom. Experiments have shown that the curious annual brood cycle of colonies in the Landes region is an adaptive, genetically based trait (Louveaux 1973, Strange et al. 2007).

Modern humans (Homo sapiens) are a recent evolutionary innovation compared to honeybees. We arose some 150,000 years ago in the African savannahs, where honeybees had already been living for eons. The earliest humans were hunter gatherers who hunted honeybees for their honey, the most delicious of all natural foods. We certainly see an appetite for honey in one hunter-gatherer people still in existence, the Hadza of northern Tanzania. Hadza men spend 4-5 hours per day in bee hunting, and honey is their favorite food (Marlowe et al. 2014).

Bee hunting began to be superseded by beekeeping some 10,000 years ago, when people in several cultures started farming and began domesticating plants and animals. Two regions where this transformation in human history occurred are the alluvial plains of Mesopotamia and the Nile Delta. In both places, ancient hive beekeeping has been documented by archaeologists. Both are within the original distribution of Apis mellifera, and both have open habitats where swarms seeking a nest site probably had difficulty finding natural cavities and occupied the clay pots and grass baskets of the early farmers (Crane 1999).

In Egypt's sun temple of King Ne-user-re at Abu Ghorab, there is a stone, bas-relief ca. 4400 years old that shows a beekeeper *kneeling by a stack of nine cylindrical clay hives. This is the earliest indication of hive beekeeping and it marks the start of our search for an optimal system of beekeeping. It also marks the start of managed colonies living in circumstances that differ markedly from the environment in which they evolved and to which they were adapted. Notice, for example, how the colonies in the hives depicted in the Egyptian bas-relief lived crowded together rather than spaced widely across the land.*

Wild Colonies vs Managed Colonies

Today there are considerable differences between the environment of evolutionary adaptation that shaped the biology of wild honeybee colonies and the current circumstances of managed honeybee colonies. Wild and managed live under different conditions because we beekeepers, like all farmers, modify the environments in which our livestock live to boost their productivity. Unfortunately, these changes in the living conditions of agricultural animals often make them more prone to pests and pathogens. In Table 1, I list 20 ways in which the living conditions of honeybees differ between wild and managed colonies, and I am sure you can think of still more.

Difference 1: *Colonies are vs. are not genetically adapted to their locations. Each of the subspecies of Apis mellifera was adapted to the climate and flora of its geographic range and each ecotype within a subspecies was adapted to a particular environment. Shipping mated queens and moving colonies long distances for migratory beekeeping forces colonies to live where they may be poorly suited. A recent, large-scale experiment conducted in Europe found that colonies with queens of local origin lived longer than colonies with queens of non-local origin (Büchler et al. 2014).*

Table 1. Comparison of the environments in which honeybee colonies lived (and sometimes still do) as wild colonies and those in which they live currently as managed colonies.

13

Environment of evolutionary adaptedness	Current circumstances
1. Colonies genetically adapted to location	Colonies not genetically adapted to location
2. Colonies live widely spaced in landscape	Colonies live crowded in apiaries
3. Colonies occupy small (ca 1.5 cu ft) cavities	Colonies occupy large (ca. 3+ cu ft) hives
4. Nest cavity walls have a propolis coating	Hive walls have no propolis coating
5. Nest cavity walls are thick (ca. 4+ in)	Hive walls are thin (ca. 3/4 in)
6. Nest entrance is high & small (ca. 4 sq in)	Nest entrance is low & large (ca. 12 sq in)
7. Nest has 10-25% drone comb	Nest has little (< 5%) drone comb
8. Nest organization is stable	Nest organization is often altered
9. Nest-site relocations are rare	Hive relocations can be frequent
10. Colonies are rarely disturbed	Colonies are frequently disturbed
11. Colonies deal with familiar diseases	Colonies deal with novel diseases
12. Colonies have diverse pollen sources	Colonies have homogeneous pollen sources
13. Colonies have natural diets	Colonies sometimes have artificial diets
14. Colonies are not exposed to novel toxins	Colonies exposed to insecticides & fungicides
15. Colonies are not treated for diseases	Colonies are treated for diseases
16. Pollen not trapped, honey not taken	Pollen sometimes trapped, honey often taken
17. Beeswax is not removed	Beeswax is removed during honey harvests
18. Bees choose larvae for queen rearing	Beekeepers choose larvae for queen rearing
19. Drones compete fiercely for mating	Queen breeder may select drones for mating
20. Drone brood not removed for mite control	Drone brood sometimes removed and frozen

Difference 2: *Colonies live widely spaced across the landscape vs. crowded in apiaries. This difference makes beekeeping practical, but it also creates a fundamental change in the ecology of honeybees. Crowded colonies experience greater competition for forage, greater risk of being robbed, and greater problems reproducing (e.g., swarms combining and queens entering wrong hives after mating). Probably the most harmful consequence of crowding colonies, though, is boosting pathogen and parasite transmission between colonies (Seeley & Smith 2015). This facilitation of disease transmission boosts the incidence of disease and it keeps alive the virulent strains of the bees' disease agents.*

Difference 3: *Colonies live in relatively small nest cavities vs. in large hives. This difference also profoundly changes the ecology of honeybees. Colonies in large hives have the space to store*

14

huge honey crops but they also swarm less because they are not as space limited, which weakens natural selection for strong, healthy colonies since fewer colonies reproduce. Colonies kept in large hives also suffer greater problems with brood parasites such as Varroa (Loftus et al. 2015).

Difference 4: *Colonies live with vs. without a nest envelope of antimicrobial plant resin. Living without a propolis envelope increases the cost of colony defense against pathogens. For example, worker in colonies without a propolis envelope invest more in costly immune system activity (i.e., synthesis of antimicrobial peptides) relative to workers in colonies with a propolis envelope (Borba et al. 2015).*

Difference 5: *Colonies have thick vs. thin nest cavity walls. This creates a difference in the energetic cost of colony thermoregulation, esp. in cold climates. The rate of heat loss for a wild colony living in a typical tree cavity is 4-7 times lower than for a managed colony living in a standard wooden hive (Mitchell 2016).*

Difference 6: *Colonies live with high and small vs. low and large entrances. This difference renders managed colonies more vulnerable to robbing and predation (large entrances are harder to guard), and it may lower their winter survival (low entrances get blocked by snow, preventing cleansing flights).*

Difference 7: *Colonies live with vs. without plentiful drone comb. Inhibiting colonies from rearing drones boosts their honey production (Seeley 2002) and slows reproduction by Varroa (Martin 1998), but it also hampers natural selection for colony health by preventing the healthiest colonies from passing on their genes (via drones) the most successfully.*

Difference 8: *Colonies live with vs. without a stable nest organization. Disruptions of nest organization for beekeeping may hinder colony functioning. In nature, honeybee colonies organize their nests with a precise 3-D organization: compact brood nest surrounded by pollen stores and honey stored above (Montovan et al. 2013). Beekeeping practices that modify the* nest organization, such as inserting empty combs to reduce congestion in the brood nest, hamper thermoregulation and may disrupt other aspects of colony functioning such as egg laying by the queen and pollen storage by foragers.

Difference 9: Colonies experience infrequent vs. sometimes frequent relocations. Whenever a colony is moved to a new location, as in migratory beekeeping, the foragers must relearn the landmarks around their hive and must discover new sources of nectar, pollen, and water. One study found that colonies moved overnight to a new location had smaller weight gains in the week following the move relative to control colonies already living in the location (Moeller 1975).

Difference 10: Colonies are rarely vs. frequently disturbed. We do not know how frequently wild colonies experience disturbances (e.g., bear attacks), but it is probably rarer than for managed colonies whose nests are easily cracked open, smoked, and manipulated. In one experiment, Taber (1963) compared the weight gains of colonies that were and were not inspected during a honey flow and found that colonies that were inspected gained 20-30% less weight (depending on extent of disturbance) than control colonies on the day of the inspections.

Difference 11: Colonies do not vs. do deal with novel diseases. Historically, honeybee colonies dealt only with the parasites and pathogens with whom they had long been in an arms race. Therefore, they had evolved means of surviving with their agents of disease. We humans changed all this when we triggered the global spread of the ectoparasitic mite Varroa destructor from eastern Asia, small hive beetle (Aethina tumida) from sub-Saharan Africa, and chalkbrood fungus (Ascosphaera apis) and acarine mite (Acarapis woodi) from Europe. The spread of Varroa alone has resulted in the deaths of millions of honeybee colonies (Martin 2012).

Difference 12: Colonies have diverse vs. homogeneous food sources. Some managed colonies are placed in agricultural ecosystems (e.g., huge almond orchards or vast fields of oilseed rape) where they experience low diversity pollen diets and poorer nutrition. The effects of pollen diversity were studied by comparing nurse bees given diets with monofloral pollens or polyfloral pollens. Bees fed the polyfloral pollen lived longer than those fed the monofloral pollens (Di Pasquale et al. 2013).

Difference 13: Colonies have natural diets vs. sometimes being fed artificial diets. Some beekeepers feed their colonies protein supplements ("pollen substitutes") to stimulate colony growth before pollen is available, to fulfill pollination contracts and produce larger honey crops. The best pollen supplements/substitutes do stimulate brood rearing, though not as well as real pollen and may result in workers of poorer quality (Scofield and Mattila 2015).

Difference 14: Colonies are not vs. are exposed to novel toxins. The most important new toxins of honeybees are insecticides and fungicides, substances for which the bees have not had time to evolve detoxification mechanisms. Honeybees are now exposed to an ever-increasing list of pesticides and fungicides that can synergize to cause harm to bees (Mullin et al. 2010).

Difference 15: Colonies are not vs. are treated for diseases. When we treat our colonies for diseases, we interfere with the host-parasite arms race between Apis mellifera and its pathogens and parasites. Specifically, we weaken natural selection for disease resistance. It is no surprise that most managed colonies in North America and Europe possess little resistance to Varroa mites, or that there are populations of wild colonies on both continents that have evolved strong resistance to these mites (Locke 2016). Treating colonies with acaricides and antibiotics may also interfere with the microbiomes of a colony's bees (Engel et al. 2016).

Difference 16: Colonies are not vs. are managed as sources of pollen and honey. Colonies managed for honey production are housed in large hives, so they are more productive. However, they are also less apt to reproduce (swarm) so there is less scope for natural selection for healthy colonies. Also, the vast quantity of brood in large-hive colonies renders them vulnerable to population explosions of *Varroa* mites and other disease agents that reproduce in brood (Loftus et al. 2015).

Difference 17: *Colonies do not vs. do suffer losses of beeswax.* Removing beeswax from a colony imposes a serious energetic burden. The weight-to-weight efficiency of beeswax synthesis from sugar is at best about 0.10 (data of Weiss 1965, analyzed in Hepburn 1986), so every pound of wax taken from a colony costs it some 10 pounds of honey that is not available for other purposes, such as winter survival. The most energetically burdensome way of harvesting honey is removal of entire combs filled with honey (e.g., cut comb honey and crushed comb honey). It is less burdensome to produce extracted honey since this removes just the capping wax.

Difference 18: *Colonies are vs. are not choosing the larvae used for rearing queens.* When we graft day-old larvae into artificial queen cups during queen rearing, we prevent the bees from choosing which larvae will develop into queens. One study found that in emergency queen rearing the bees do not choose larvae at random and instead favor those of certain patrilinies (Moritz et al. 2005).

Difference 19: *Drones are vs. are not allowed to compete fiercely for mating.* In bee breeding programs that use artificial insemination, the drones that provide sperm do not have to prove their vigor by competing amongst other drones for mating. This weakens the sexual selection for drones that possess genes for health and strength.

Difference 20: *Drone brood is not vs. is removed from colonies for mite control.* The practice of removing drone brood from colonies to control *Varroa destructor* partially castrates colonies and so interferes with natural selection for colonies that are healthy enough to invest heavily in drone production.

Suggestions for Darwinian Beekeeping

Beekeeping looks different from an evolutionary perspective. We see that colonies of honeybees lived independently from humans for millions of years, and during this time they were shaped by natural selection to be skilled at surviving and reproducing wherever they lived, in Europe, western Asia, or Africa. We also see that ever since humans started keeping bees in hives, we have been disrupting the exquisite fit that once existed between honeybee colonies and their environments. We've done this in two ways: 1) by moving colonies to geographical locations to which they are not well adapted, and 2) by managing colonies in ways that interfere with their lives but that provide us with honey, beeswax, propolis, pollen, Royal Jelly, and pollination services.

What can we do, as beekeepers, to help honeybee colonies live with a better fit to their environment, and thereby live with less stress and better health? The answer to this question depends greatly on how many colonies you manage, and what you want from your bees. A beekeeper who has a few colonies and low expectations for honey crops, for example, is in a vastly different situation than a beekeeper who has thousands of colonies and is earning a living through beekeeping.

For those interested, I offer 10 suggestions for bee-friendly beekeeping. Some have general application while others are feasible only for the backyard beekeeper.

1. *Work with bees that are adapted to your location. For example, if you live in New England, buy queens and nucs produced up north rather than queens and packages shipped up from the south. Or, if you live in a location where there are few beekeepers, use bait hives to capture swarms from the wild colonies living in your area. (Incidentally, these swarms will build you beautiful new combs, and this will enable you to retire old combs that could have heavy loads of pesticide residues and pathogen spores/cells.) The key thing is to acquire queens of a stock that is adapted to your climate.*

2.   *Space your hives as widely as possible. Where I live, in central New York State, there are vast forests filled with wild honeybee colonies spaced roughly a half mile apart. This is perhaps ideal for wild colonies but problematic for the beekeeper. Still, spacing colonies just 30-50 yards apart in an apiary greatly reduces drifting and thus the spread of disease.*

3.   *House your bees in small hives. Consider using just one deep hive body for a brood nest and one medium-depth super over a queen excluder for honey. You won't harvest as much honey, but you will likely have reduced disease and pest problems, particularly Varroa. And yes, your colonies will swarm, but swarming is natural and research shows that it promotes colony health by helping keep Varroa mite populations at safe levels (see Loftus et al 2015).*

4.   *Roughen the inner walls of your hives or build them of rough-sawn lumber. This will stimulate your colonies to coat the interior surfaces of their hives with propolis, thereby creating antimicrobial envelopes around their nests.*

5.   *Use hives whose walls provide good insulation. These might be hives built of thick lumber, or they might be hives made of plastic foam. We urgently need research on how much insulation is best for colonies in different climates, and how it is best provided.*

6.   *Position hives high off the ground. This is not always doable, but if you have a porch or deck where you can position some hives, then perhaps it is feasible. We urgently need research on how much entrance height is best in different climates.*

7.   *Let 10-20% of the comb in your hives be drone comb. Giving your colonies the opportunity to rear drones can help improve the genetics in your area. Drones are costly, so it is only the strongest and healthiest colonies that can*

afford to produce legions of drones. Unfortunately, drone brood also fosters rapid growth of a colony's population of Varroa mites, so providing plentiful drone comb requires careful monitoring of the Varroa levels in your hives (see suggestion 10, below).

8. *Minimize disturbances of nest organization. When working a colony, replace each frame in its original position and orientation. Also, avoid inserting empty frames in the brood nest to inhibit swarming.*

9. *Minimize relocations of hives. Move colonies as rarely as possible. If you must do so, then do so when there is little forage available.*

10. *Refrain from treating colonies for Varroa. WARNING: This last suggestion should only be adopted if you can do so carefully, as part of a program of extremely diligent beekeeping. If you pursue treatment-free beekeeping without close attention to your colonies, then you will create a situation in your apiary in which natural selection is favoring virulent Varroa mites, not Varroa-resistant bees. To help natural selection favor Varroa-resistant bees, you will need to monitor closely the mite levels in all your colonies and kill those whose mite populations are skyrocketing long before these colonies can collapse. By preemptively killing your Varroa-susceptible colonies, you will accomplish two important things: 1) you will eliminate your colonies that lack Varroa resistance and 2) you will prevent the "mite bomb" phenomenon of mites spreading en masse to your other colonies. If you don't perform these preemptive killings, then even your most resistant colonies could become overrun with mites and die, which means that there will be no natural selection for mite resistance in your apiary. Failure to perform preemptive killings can also spread virulent mites to your neighbors' colonies and even to the wild colonies in your area that are slowly evolving resistance on their own. If you are not willing to kill your*

mite-susceptible colonies, then you will need to treat them and requeen them with a queen of mite-resistant stock.

Two Hopes

> "As someone who has devoted his scientific career to investigating the marvelous workings of honeybee colonies, it saddens me to see how profoundly – and ever increasingly – conventional beekeeping disrupts and endangers the lives of colonies."
>
> Thomas D. Seeley

I hope you have found it useful to think about beekeeping from an evolutionary perspective. If you are interested in pursuing beekeeping in a way that is centered less on treating a bee colony as a honey factory, and more on nurturing the lives of honeybees, then I encourage you to consider what I call Darwinian Beekeeping. Others call it Natural Beekeeping, Apicentric Beekeeping, and Bee-friendly Beekeeping (Phipps 2016). Whatever the name, its practitioners view a honeybee colony as a complex bundle of adaptations shaped by natural selection to maximize a colony's survival and reproduction in competition with other colonies and other organisms (predators, parasites, and pathogens). It seeks to foster colony health by letting the bees live as naturally as possible, so they can make full use of the toolkit of adaptations that they have acquired over the last 30 million years. Much remains to be learned about this toolkit. How exactly do colonies benefit from better nest insulation? Do colonies tightly seal their nests with propolis in autumn to have an in-hive water supply (condensate) over winter? How exactly do colonies benefit from having a high nest entrance? The methods of Darwinian Beekeeping are still being developed, but fortunately, apicultural research is starting to embrace a Darwinian perspective (Neumann and Blacquière 2016).

I hope too that you will consider giving Darwinian Beekeeping a try, for you might find it more enjoyable than conventional beekeeping., especially if you are a small-scale beekeeper. Everything is done with bee-friendly intentions and in ways that harmonize with the natural history of Apis mellifera. As someone who has devoted his scientific career to investigating the marvelous inner workings of honey colonies, it saddens me to see how profoundly -and ever increasingly- conventional beekeeping disrupts and endangers the lives of colonies. Darwinian Beekeeping, which integrates respecting the bees and using them for practical purposes, seems to me like a good way to be responsible keepers of these small creatures, our greatest friends among the insects. Acknowledgements and References of Seeley's article may be viewed within the articles listed earlier.

If you're interested in more of Tom Seeley on Darwinian Beekeeping, you may purchase his book, Following the Wild Bees: The Craft and Science of Bee Hunting, *which includes his talks at Bee Audacious, a unique working conference where bee experts, beekeepers, farmers, community organizers, and more come together to envision bold, evidence-based solutions to help honeybees, wild bees, beekeepers, and pollination managers prosper. See picture to the right.*

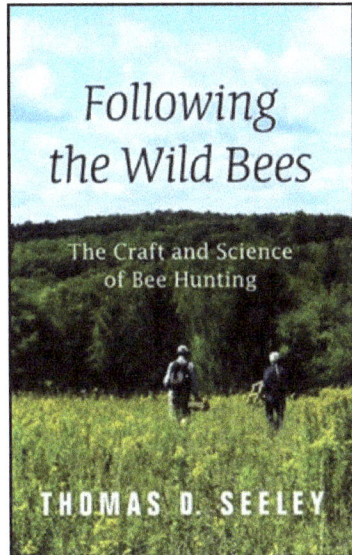

Though my views on Varroa are different and will be discussed later, I was impressed that a scientist would come to my way of thinking on working with honeybees.

2: Why BEe Perspective

Photo: TalkingWithBees.com

Beekeeping is a wondrous, beautiful, fulfilling hobby, if *hobby* is the appropriate word. Nurturing parents want to think their way is the best way and usually have no problems telling you so. You can keep honeybees for the joy of watching the flying little wonders pollinate your garden, flowers, all your plants. Be aware though, it takes a commitment to keep bees, especially on their terms because it is so hard to not include your ego.

Keeping bees is not the same as keeping a pet. When you're away from home, you can take your pet to a kennel or leave it with a sitter. Bees are not that easy, especially if you have more than 10 hives. You can plan on spending a lot of time with them in the spring if you want to expand your apiary by splitting your colonies. Splitting your own bee colonies is creating false swarms. You will have a few days of free time, but you will have to put the split into its permanent home and watch it for a week or so and feed it if the bees don't have enough food.

For the past few years, people are looking at the massive deaths of honeybees and want to do what they can to help them. They go out and buy bees and equipment, set them up, then sit back and watch them or work the bees the way they think is best. Beekeeping has dramatically changed from 30 years ago. After what could be a $500 investment, the uneducated beekeeper will more often than not lose their bees. They get discouraged, give up, and give away their equipment, not knowing if the equipment is diseased.

Besides getting the ego out of the way, the main premise of BEe Perspective Beekeeping is keeping the bees from being stressed which is caused by many factors. Stress is usually the number one cause of an unhealthy hive because stress compromises the bees' immune systems. Knowing what stresses the colony will help you to know what to do and what not to do.

Below are tactics that many beekeepers have used that is not in alignment with BEe Perspective Beekeeping.

Treating with Chemicals

Beekeeping has become so commercialized on such a large scale, it boggles the mind. Commercial beekeepers move bees throughout the year over thousands of miles to pollinate monocrops. They use harsh chemicals like Coumophas[iv] (CheckMite+™) and fluvalinate (Apistan®)[v] to treat Varroa mites. While these are only two chemicals, there are also many others that are suspected to be the cause of high supersedure rates (bees killing the old queen and making new queens). Both chemicals are fat-soluble and with repeated use will accumulate in the wax and honey, which over time will affect the bees' health. These chemicals are also known to cause infertility in drones and queens. According to DNA, the mites, *Varroa jacobsoni,* seen in the 1980s are different from the mites we have today.[vi] Today the mites are called Varroa *destructors*, or just mites.

Natural or organic beekeepers are using essential oils, often referred to as *soft chemicals*. These oils interfere with the queen's pheromones, thereby interfering with the hive's ability to communicate, stressing the hive. If not removed in a timely manner, the oils on the strips will invade the honey and wax which are both non-polar (they draw oils). Curiously, honey is also polar (it draws water). If the chemical strips are still in the hive, it may also mean the bees have lost the intellectual ability to remove that which is not part of their natural habitat. This is also one of the issues with the honeybees' diluted gene pool.

The chemicals, be they soft or harsh, are unnatural and are part of the reasons for sick bees. Using them without actually knowing what the issue is synonymous to giving your child antibiotics as a preventive medicine. In time, their bodies become resistant, and stronger antibiotics may be needed when they do get sick. It's the same with bees. Chemicals not only affect the bacterial balance in the hive, they affect the bees' autoimmune systems. And then there is the idea of the combination of the chemicals affecting the hive. It is much better the grow the plants like oregano, lavender, lemon balm, thyme ... and allow the bees to take in what they need through their honey.

It is easy to train bees because it is an animal. If a hive is accustomed to treatments for pests and diseases, the colony will most likely die without the treatments. This is one of the reasons why feral bees have survived longer than domesticated bees. They have learned to survive without human intervention.

Combining Hives

Two of the hardest things for people to do is to *accept* and to *let go*. On a deeper level, they are both the same. People have a hard time accepting when a thing is ready to die with dignity. If there is a lot of space in the hive and the colony is showing weakness, it's best to put the hive into a nuc box. Bees like small, tight spaces and when they get ill or weak will feel overwhelmed in large spaces. If the colony stays weak for whatever reason, it may be best to let it die. I will not support a weak hive because the weakness can be a disease of which I am unaware or cannot see. It could also be weak genetics that I have seen in some of the packages of bees. I do not believe in death as defined in our dictionaries. The two Laws of thermodynamics have proven that energy doesn't die, nor is it created. It just changes. Death is the same thing. The body goes back to the earth that nourished and sustained it, and its essence goes back to its origin. Bees are no different.

Mother doesn't combine hives, and I wouldn't recommend it either. If that weak hive is allowed to live, it usually spreads the weakness to other hives – especially if you combine it with a stronger hive. You don't see honeybees crowding into another occupied hive because they no longer have one or don't like the hive they were living in. They will swarm to another location. Mind you, there may be exceptions.

Weakening the Gene Pool

There are only a handful of commercial queen rearers in the United States. Their queens mate with the same species of drones in the same yard year after year, which could be weakening the gene pool. A weakened gene pool does not give the honeybees a chance of survival in an environment of chemical sprays, bad beekeeping, and being transported several thousands of miles for pollination purposes.

Usually, when most beekeepers make splits, they usually leave their new splits in the same area as the original hive. If there are many hives in the same location, it may not be an issue. But if you have only one or two hives, you are risking the bees' mating with their cousins or siblings – especially if both original hives came from the same source. Diverse genetics is another way of assuring a strong lineage in your colony. Mutts are highly intelligent.

Using Diseased Equipment

I consider myself a courageous individual, but jumping into beekeeping without education is unreasonable to me, especially if you don't have a lot of money to waste. I saw bee equipment at the dump and learned that a couple had purchased the equipment and bees without any knowledge of beekeeping. When their bees died, they got discouraged and threw everything away. I almost picked them up until I remembered what was said in bee school. I learned to never use or purchase used bee equipment unless I knew the beekeeper personally.

Failing to Feed Properly

I have never been able to understand why a beekeeper would take all the honey from a hive and then feed sugar water. Time and effort are money, and it would cost less if they had left enough honey for the bees to survive. Plus, there are no nutrients in sugar water. Its pH level is 7.0 which is good for growing mold. If fed in the fall, this creates Nosema the following spring. Instead, the beekeeper could have used apple cider vinegar (ACV) to bring the sugar water feed down to the acidic 4.0 to 4.3 pH that is in honey; then add a little honey for some nutrients and allow the good bacteria (*Lactobacilli*) to grow for optimum health. Honey provides the right nutrients and bacteria for honeybees. When they are fed properly, they will not have Nosema come spring, which is when it is prevalent when there are not enough *Lactobacilli* (probiotics) in the hive's food stores. Nosema disappears once the bees are able to gather fresh nectar in the spring because this bacterium is in everything in nature.

Bees have all the good bacteria in their stomachs that are needed for a healthy immune system. The honey added to the sugar formula with the ACV at room temperature will multiply the good bacteria through a fermentation process. The recipe is in the formula section of this book. I give the formula to my bees whenever my neighbors use Roundup® which is at least twice per year. Glyphosate – such as that in Roundup®, as well as Rodeo® used by utility companies, and other herbicides – kill the *Lactobacilli* that is required by all living elements on the earth for a good immune system.

The other formula is adding a capsule of *Lactobacilli* with 10 strains at 30 billion colony-forming units (CFUs) to a cup of tepid water and then putting two tablespoons of this probiotic water into a gallon of feed. I use this for European Foulbrood (EFB) which is brought on by stress. Once the farmers and others start spraying glyphosate in their fields, yards, or around fences, *Lactobacilli* will disappear except in the natural or organic farms or yards. Understand, though, Roundup® will travel in the wind for miles and miles until it rains and then it goes into the ground. This topic will be covered more in the disease section of this book.

These formulas are the only exceptions to the treatment-free rule. Though, I don't consider them treatments as defined by beekeepers, but, rather giving back to the bees what is destroyed through chemical sprays.

Pollinating Crops

Bee colonies and their hives were not designed to travel across town or across country to pollinate a monocrop. It takes more than just several nucs to replenish the hives that die during transportation. The beekeeper makes good money by charging a large price per hive, but the cost of an accident like the ones shown in the picture on the previous page is not

worth the cost of dead bees. When semi-trucks spill hive equipment and bees across the highway, the bees will need to be killed because they have become hazardous to the public. This whole practice of mobile pollination is sad.

I always advocate those in agriculture should pay someone to tend to the bees and keep them in the area. But then I see miles and miles of monocultures and get concerned about this whole scenario. Honeybees need a polyculture for survival.

Feral Bees

Dr. Deborah Delaney, University of Delaware, did a study on feral bees (published 2014).[vii] I met Dr. Delaney in 2012 and became fascinated with her work. Below is an excerpt of her study on why feral bees survive pests and diseases:

> "Colonies living in the wild rely on their inherent abilities to resist diseases, which drive selection for disease resistance, whereas colonies kept by beekeepers often receive antibiotic or pesticide treatments, which blunt selection for disease resistance. Also, colonies living in the wild are dispersed over the landscape, whereas colonies managed by beekeepers are crowded in apiaries. When colonies are widely separated, their parasites and pathogens are probably transmitted mostly vertically (from parent colony to offspring colony) through swarming, but when living side by side in apiaries, their disease agents are easily transmitted horizontally (between unrelated colonies) through drifting and robbing behaviors (Pfeiffer and Crailsheim 1998; Seeley and Smith in press). Therefore, when honeybee colonies live under natural conditions, it is likely that their parasites and pathogens will be selected to be avirulent, for this will enable their hosts to stay healthy and produce the swarms needed to transmit the parasites and pathogens to new colonies (Fries and Camazine 2001; Schmid-Hempel 2011)."

I understood that a feral hive had to be documented for three years to be designated feral. Since learning about feral hives and doing my own research in my apiaries, I have learned to have the bees show me how they can live as feral bees. I don't go into my hives as often as other beekeepers, and I allow the bees to fend for themselves as though they were living in trees. I don't put on honey supers with the intentions of harvesting that honey for myself. My experience thus far has been that after the first year, the colony takes on the characteristic traits of a feral hive. The traits I found are:

- Their cluster gets smaller.
- They sometimes swarm, but not always, especially if they have the room.
- They are stingy with the honey by collecting just enough for themselves. Sometimes there is extra for me.
- Sometimes a hive will start out tame then turn a little aggressive. I don't know if the change is because I don't go into the hive often or not. The whole idea of a domestic hive turning feral is a little bit of a mystery for me. But I do think it could be that they revert back to the wild state when not bothered too often or treated with chemicals, gadgets, or traps.

3: Bee Equipment You'll Need

While traveling in Senegal, Africa, I visited with my two foster sons, Jean and Andre, in Dakar. Several days later we went to Nemending and visited their uncle Leon Ndiaye. Leon is a bushman who coiled his hive out of natural grass. You will see his colorful hive later in this book. The next day, we met with a couple of the beekeepers in the bush and inspected large cement hives that were about three feet long and about 20 inches wide. It took a strong African to open the heavy cement lid. The problem was that each hive was placed on stacked tires. When the lid was removed, the hive rocked and the bees went wild. While it was winter for us, it was the end of rainy season for them with temperatures in the mid-70s. But the bees behaved similar to those in our geographic area in the winter time. They were not at all happy when we opened their hive at that time of year.

I watched in disbelief as the African beekeeper used his hands to aggressively brush the bees off the frames. I grabbed the tool from his hand and asked my translator to translate. I showed him, and the other beekeepers with him, how to use the tool and the slow pace at which to use it. After a few minutes, the bees quieted down and moved to the opposite end of where I was working, as seen in the picture on the next page. Though the beekeepers were impressed, they unfortunately forgot about my instructions when we went to the next hive. The zipper on my suit had worked open about a half inch and 19 bees found their way into the tiny gap. When I arrived back at my host's residence, his wife, Therese kept clicking her tongue and saying I needed to go the hospital.

A couple days later, we were told of a swarm near a farm filled with women and children laborers. My two adopted sons, I and a couple of others suited up and went looking for the swarm. Half way to the field, I looked back and saw Leon walking behind us with his hand behind his back. I chuckled when I realized why he hadn't suited up. By the time we reached the field, we spotted the scorch mark on the large limb of a tree on the edge of the field. The farm hands had taken a torch to the swarm of bees. When I saw the scorch mark on the limb, I shook my head at their ignorance and explained how swarming bees don't bother humans while in the process of finding another home. But then, Leon knew this.

On the way back to his home, I again laughed and shook my head at the idea of getting swept up in the moment and forgot about swarming bees not stinging. When we got to the shade tree in the center of the yard, my host put on his bee suit and left. About 30 minutes later he came back with a rather large basket containing a quart-sized honeycomb with bees on it. He plopped the basket down alongside me and the nearby children ran. I shouted back at them for them to see that I was still seated next to the basket of honeycomb and bees, unafraid. I knew the bees were busy with the honey and wouldn't bother with us. When the kids saw all this, they came closer and even dared to finger out a little honey.

I gave Leon an inquisitive look while he stepped out of his suit. He responded, "I knew if you weren't afraid, there was no reason for me to be afraid."

Beehive Bodies

I enjoy unusual hives, including observation hives. The fact is, the bees will swarm into anything if they feel there is enough space. A friend told me about one of his swarms going into a black plastic bag and living there for two months until his son moved the swarm to a hive box. Whether one hive is better than the other will depend on the beekeeper's taste and his or her beekeeping practices. On the next few pages are different types of hives.

Ancient Beehives of Tree Trunk & Straw

Long Langstroth as Top Bar
http://horizontalhive.com/how-to-build/long-langstroth-plans.shtml

Leon, A Senegalese bushman with his handwoven beehive.

Author's Traditional Langstroth

Variation of Warre Hive
Photo: warre.biobees.com/hexagon.htm

Observation Hive
Photo: http://www.bushfarms.com /beesobservationhives.htm

British National
Photo: Hivehttp://www.peak- ives.co.uk/page/4/

36

Beekeeping Tools

I do make my own entrance covers, as pictured to the right, because I enjoy watching the forager bees pass off the honey to the house bees through the ¼-inch wire mesh. The bees like to hang out behind the screen during hot, humid days.

Among the many different types of tools my favorites for inspections are:

Standard Hive Tool

Frame Cleaner
especially for the grooves for when you are replacing the comb

Maxant J Hook Hive Tool
assists in lifting frames out of the hive

Frame Gripper

do not get the pointed ones; they tend to dig in below the frame and tear comb

Frame Perch

this is a must

Bee Brush

may come in handy

Sometimes, folks use a feather to brush the bees because it is not as harsh as a brush. Others use their breath to blow the bees away. Bees don't like human breath unless the individual is diabetic as they do like the sweet sugar smell.

Always get tools that suit your needs best. If you live in an area where there are Africanized bees, you will probably need a full jump suit. In my area, I sometimes use only a veil. Depending on the bee species, I may use a jacket with the veil.

Full suit
Photo: Kelley Bee Supply

Jacket with veil
Photo: Kelley Bee Supply

In my list of tools, you will notice the absence of a smoker because I don't use one. It coats the wax making the smoke odor last longer. More importantly, the smoke interferes with the hive's ability to spread pheromones for the purpose of communication. The bees are so busy dealing with the smoke, they cannot communicate with you. However, being taught by a mentor, it is often the preference of the beekeeper to use one. If you feel you need something to calm the bees, put a little sugar in a bottle of water and lightly spritz the bees. They will usually go to the task of grooming each other and allow you to do your inspection.

Beehive Bodies and Frames

A beekeeper has the option of working with a 10-frame hive or 8-frame Langstroth hive or topbar hives. I prefer 8-frame because the bees like small, tight places, and it is easier for me to lift the full boxes. Getting older I found that having an extra box in the field allowed me to divide the frames in the boxes to make them lighter. I just place the frames back in the same place in the hive as I finish the inspection.

There are a variety of screened or solid bottom boards, different styles of medium boxes used for honey supers or brood, large boxes used for brood, and variations of inner screened or solid cover, and variations of top telescoping covers. You can work with different mentors to discern which kind of hive body fits your beekeeping style. The queen usually doesn't lay above 18" so I never found the need for a queen excluder to prevent her from laying in the honey supers above the brood box. I have seen where the excluder has torn the wings of workers moving through either the plastic or metal parts.

Wooden frames are used for all my hives. Some beekeepers will use wired foundations because it's easier. I don't use them because the wire retains the extreme hot and cold temperatures.

4.9 mm Foundation

For my brood nest, I prefer the 4.9 mm foundation and feel it is the best cell size to help control the *Varroa destructor*. While visiting Cra Api bee lab in Bologna, Italy, I was given a study done in 1998[viii] regarding 4.9 mm cells. The cells are supposedly capped off a day sooner so the mites are less apt to lay their eggs on the bee larvae. Curious thing about evolution, the Varroa will adapt; but so may the honeybees. By the time the Varroa have figured out the timeframe of the 4.9 mm cell, the hygienic bees will have learned to bite off the mite's legs and either drop them through the screened bottom board or take the mite body out the entrance.

I use a ¾-inch piece of 4.9-millimeter (mm) foundation strip cut about 6-inches long, placed in the groove under the top of the frame and held in place by a couple drops of melted beeswax. The bees will complete the seal. The strip is to assure the bees will build the wax straight across rather than several teardrop shapes spaced askew across the frame.

Deep and medium frames usually have four holes in the sides of the frame. I use 40-pound nylon fishing line to string the line in the second hole from the top and through the last hole toward the bottom of the frame. Bees don't always build comb to the bottom of the frame, so the line placed in the last hole will ensure support during inspections and honey extractions. Tie the line with a square knot and a regular knot on the outside of the frame next to a hole. After you cut off the excess line, try to pull the knot through the nearest hole. I don't like the idea of my girls tearing their wings on the cut end of the fishing line when moving around on the side of the frame.

The bees adapt to this nylon line far better than metal. You can remove the fishing line on old combs by cutting the line at the opposite side of the knot and then holding onto the knot, pulling the line through the holes of the frame. The line usually comes cleanly through the honeycomb. Fishing line is one of the few exceptions to my statement, "If they don't take it through the entrance, I don't put it through the roof."

NOTE: It takes 10 pounds of honey, about the weight of a full deep frame, to make one pound of wax. So, commercial beekeepers reuse the wax foundation rather than have the bees make new. Considering what few drams it takes to make a foundation for one frame, you can get a lot of frames of honeycomb out of 10 pounds of honey. Since commercial wax has over 250 kinds of chemicals, it will be a lot healthier for the bees and you if the bees make their own wax, especially for the honey super.

HOUSEL POSITION FOR FOUNDATION

Beekeeper Michael Housel discovered the position of how bees built the honeycombs in the hive. When I first heard of this, I checked a box of dead bees killed by wasps. The frames were foundationless when I put them in the hive because I had nothing else. I checked the honeycombs, and he was right.

He states that starting from the center of the hive the bees build the honeycombs with the standard Y facing the outer walls and the inverted (upside down) Y facing the center.[ix] The center of the hive box is when you divide the amount of an 8-frame or 10-frame Langstroth in half, with either four or five frames on either side of center. Put the comb up against the sunlight and look for the rhomboid, which is what the bottom of the comb is called. These can be seen in an old comb either at the bottom or in the corners of the frame.

Standard Y
faces the wall

Y is center of rhomboid

Inverted Y
faces the center

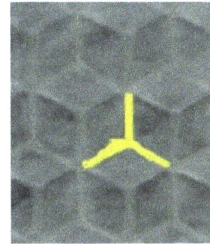

Depending on what company you purchase your frames, there is a detachable piece of lathing under the top of the frame that you cut off by sliding a utility knife along the groove. Take off the lath and clean the excess wood off of it and the frame where it was attached. If you use wax foundation with wire support, check the top of the foundation for the curved elbow part of the wire.

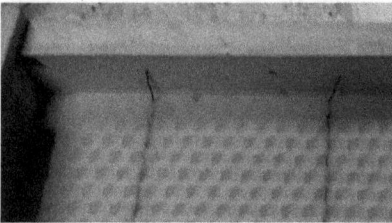

Gently push the bottom part of the foundation into the grooves of the bottom of the frame. Lay the foundation down on the frame so that the bent wires face up and will lie under the lathing.

Place the lathing piece back on top of the wire and nail in place with ½ inch brad nails or use an air compressor. If you look at the foundation with the removable lathing facing you, you will see that the foundation has been placed with the inverted Y facing you and the other side of the comb will show the standard Y.

All wax foundation is pressed and the wire added on the side of the inverted Y. The Y is actually the cell wall on the other side of the foundation. Checking for the removable lathing at the top of the frame, you will know it is placed correctly in the frame. It will also indicate how to place the frame back into the hive.

Simply put: to determine how to use the Housel Position when putting in foundationless frames, I have the frames with the detachable lath piece at the top of the frame facing the center of the hive box.

This sounds tedious, but I do it because the bees do it. I think, too, that the way the foundation is pressed indicates that the companies forming the foundation are also aware of the Housel Position. It may be confusing when you first start, but after a couple inspections, you will understand. To check, I deliberately placed a frame back in the box in a different way and the increased buzzing noise indicated the bees were not happy.

Most beekeepers don't use the Housel Position and some will say it makes no difference. Perhaps this is true, but I have found that my bees are happier when I follow their organizational habits.

PLASTIC FRAMES

I don't recommend plastic frames as they are harmful to honeybees. The following information is detailed because I want you to understand what you are giving your bees when you use anything plastic in the beehive, especially the foundation. You will also learn what you are feeding yourselves when drinking from plastic bottles and straws, cooking or reheating in plastic in microwave ovens, or storing food in non-food grade plastic. Even Styrofoam emits a cancerous toxic fume when heated.

There are seven types of plastics[x/xi] that describe a group of chemicals called polymers. Heating hydrocarbons (oil, natural gas, or coal) produces plastics. This process is called cracking because a catalyst is used to break larger molecules into smaller ones. The smaller molecules are those such as ethylene (ethane), C_2H_4; propylene (propene), C_3H_6; butane, C_4H_8; and other hydrocarbons. These chemicals, as well as styrene, are called monomers. Patent #US3088135 references what plastic frames are made of.[xii]

> "While reference has been made to plastic as forming the basis of the material for constructing the comb foundation, it is to be understood that this includes such material as polyethylene plastics, acrylic plastics, and

other resinous or synthetic plastics, and other permanent, non-metallic foundation material which is acceptable to bees for building comb cells thereon, either with or without being coated with a wax or other material acceptable to the bees."

These frames are sprayed with hot wax. To get wax to the point of using it as a thin coating or pouring, it needs to be 160°F to 180°F. If beeswax is heated above 185°F, discoloration occurs. The flash point of beeswax is 400°F.

Plastic frames contain some of the same plastic used to make plastic drinking bottles that will expose antimony, a cancer-causing agent, at different temperatures.[xiii]

The National Geographic also reported the dangers of harmful chemicals in plastic.[xiv]

"The scientists simulated the decomposition of polystyrene in the sea and found that it degraded at temperatures of 86°F (30°C). Left behind in the water were the same compounds detected in the ocean samples, such as styrene trimer, a polystyrene by-product, and bisphenol A, a chemical used in hard plastics such as reusable water bottles and the linings of aluminum cans. Bisphenol A (BPA) has been shown to interfere with the reproductive systems of animals, while styrene monomer is a suspected carcinogen. The pollutants are likely to be more concentrated in areas heavily littered with plastic debris, such as ocean vortices, which occur where currents meet. Don't drink water from plastic bottles left in a hot place for a long time. Chemicals in plastics, mainly antimony (Sb) and Bisphenol A (BPA) can leach into any liquid in a plastic bottle, according to new research, and those chemicals can potentially cause diseases (such as cancer) when consumed, based on other research."

Plastic frames were invented in the 1960s and have been used in beekeeping since that time. Later, in 2006, Herbert Drapkin was approved for the invention of adding plastic pellets to wax to create the artificial plastic honeycomb for beehive foundations. Everything was good until 2017.

On April 25, 2017, the National Public Radio (NPR) had a program on *Galleria mellonella*, commonly known as a wax worm and is the same Greater Wax Moth that will enter a weak beehive and eat the comb. The article does not state if the wax moth eats the plastic or if the moth's gut bacteria is digesting it.[xv] My question is, "Did the wax moth evolve from eating plastic foundation in beehives?" All things evolve to survive in their environment.

OLD FRAMES

Bee propolize the honeycomb cell rather than clean it out. Adding the combined chemicals that are brought in from everywhere in our environment, the comb can become filled with harmful substances. For this reason, it is recommended that you change out your frames of old wax every four to five years. It can be difficult to know which year each frame was put into the hive, so the beekeeping community has come up with an easy system to identify the years.

COLOR CODES

The chart on the next page is used to mark queens so that a beekeeper knows how old their queen is.

You can use this same chart to mark your frames with the corresponding year with flat colored thumb tacks pushed into the top front of the frame. It is hard to get rid of paint or permanent markers. Placing the thumb tack at the top of the frame that faces the front of the hive will also help to show you how to put the frame back into the hive during inspections.

International Queen Marking Color

COLOR	FOR YEAR ENDING IN:
White (or Gray)	1 or 6
Yellow	2 or 7
Red	3 or 8
Green	4 or 9
Blue	5 or 0

4: A New Home for Your Bees

Locating Your Apiary

Your bees need at least seven or more hours of sunlight a day. With too much shade, the bees will develop chalkbrood or stonebrood (fungi borne of too much humidity and mold). Bees also need lots of room between hives and between rows of hives. Think of how they like to live in their environment up in the trees. They like to have their home as much by themselves as they can. In a 16x16 square foot area, there should be no more than eight hives with walking room all the way around the hive stands. You can place four hives on an 8-foot stand with space between hives one and two and a space between hives three and four. Hives two and three are side-by-side. The space between the front and back row should be about 8-feet or more. If possible, stagger the front and back hives where the entrances aren't impeded by the hive in front. The goal is to keep them from having to fly over a hive and dive-bomb into their own hives with a harvest load.

You will hear folks say the bees need to face the east or southeast, but they will find the sun no matter where the entrance is. When I visited Dr. John Kefus on his country farm near Toulouse, France, I saw his hives on the ground with the backs of four single boxes of National 10-frame hives in a square pattern where the entrances face each of the four directions. There were no problems. The honey had already been harvested by the time I visited him in October, so none of his hives had more than one brood box on a solid bottom board that sat on the ground. His setup went against everything I was taught in beekeeping.

The hive location should have some shade against the hot west sun and some protection from harsh winds. Water source is crucial as the bees use it for temperature control. Unless you plan to give water on a daily basis, you should place the apiary near a stream or creek or some other source of clean water.

Let's not forget the nectar source. If you have a large enough space, plant plenty of perennial bee plants: annuals, vegetables, trees (including fruit), shrubs, and especially herbs. Preferably, you want plants blooming throughout the growing season. Plant anything and everything you think a bee will like for nectar, pollen, and propolis; select plants not invasive or poisonous to pets and humans. Bees are not fond of hybrid plants, and GMO crops can kill them. Check with your local or state agricultural office, or just research the internet for bee plants in your area. I plant medicinal plants for my bees – especially mints and thymes. I also planted two Bee Bee trees (*Tetradium daniellii*). When it bloomed the first time, I had no idea there were so many teeny, tiny pollinators in our area. Everything seemed to be on those trees, including several varieties of bees and butterflies.

The idea is to get the natural oils from mints, thymes, and wild plants into the honey which will add medicinal doses of healing elements for you, the bees, and pest control.

Using Geomagnetic Lines

A beekeeper friend from Rome asked me if I had heard of Ley Lines:

"Ley lines /leɪ laɪnz/ are apparent alignments of land forms, places of ancient religious significance or culture, often including man-made structures. They are ancient, straight 'paths' or routes in the landscape which are believed to have spiritual significance. The phrase was coined in 1921 by the amateur archaeologist Alfred Watkins, referring to supposed alignments of numerous places of geographical and historical interest, such as ancient monuments and megaliths, natural ridge-tops and water-fords. In his books Early British Trackways and The Old Straight Track, he sought to identify ancient trackways in the British landscape. Watkins later developed theories that these alignments were created for ease of overland trekking by line-of-sight navigation during Neolithic times and had persisted in the landscape over millennia." [xvi]

Doing more research, I came across John Harding,[xvii] A professional 36-year master beekeeper (now retired) from the UK. John explained what he terms *geomagnetic lines* in the earth. With permission, John allowed me to share some of his experience.

"… groundbreaking work in finding a natural reason for the demise proved by the relevance of a statement by Nikola Tesla who said over 100 years ago: "The day science begins to study non-physical phenomena; it will make more progress in one decade than in all the previous centuries of its existence." Nikola Tesla, 1856-1943.

I feel I have found the link to a crucial survival phenomenon for honeybees that is invisible to the human eye which affects all life and every organism on Planet Earth.'

During his years of beekeeping, John learned the following:

- *Varroa destructor* is no longer a problem for honeybees.

- More honey is produced.

- Less swarms.

- No empty hive bodies could be found.

- All bait swarm boxes are full.

Since 1992, John:

> *"... has not used chemicals of any sort hoping one day to find a natural answer to the honeybee demise using his 300 beehives as a barometer. Many years of success, failures and heartache, my dreams have been fulfilled. When I found the discovery, many questions were answered as to why many 20-year-old colonies were thriving and are not dying with no explanation as to why in the early years although the parasitic mite, Varroa destructor was being kept to a minimum or zero. I also discovered supersedure was more common than swarming and producing 2-3 times more honey when in the correct position of what honeybees want."*

After reading John's book, *Geomagnetic Honeybee,* I again did more research and found that Ley lines are the paths on the earth's surface where the ground below the surface has been broken with underground water streams, otherwise known as geomagnetic lines. These underground streams have particles in the water that magnify the earth's electrical hertz from 190 to 250 Hz. Our ancestors and animals had the ability to intuit these lines.

These energetic lines can be as far down a few hundred feet below the surface and can be felt as high as 30,000 feet into the air. The migratory birds use these lines as a navigational means of flying from one place to another. Cats love these lines, but dogs do not.

When we first walked our property, I came across a 4-inch hole in the ground where a stream could be heard and I saw the water rapidly flowing like a tiny creek about 12 inches below the surface. I live in a community where creeks and streams are all over the mountains, so it is logical to have springs below ground containing contaminants, metal, or other particles in the water that magnify the water's electrical hertz. Oak trees and elderberry bushes grow above these lines, and the water under them are usually the reason lightning strikes them first and why bees will swarm to them.

On our website, BEeHealingGuild.org, is my blog entitled *Our Electrical Mother* which explains how everything that exists

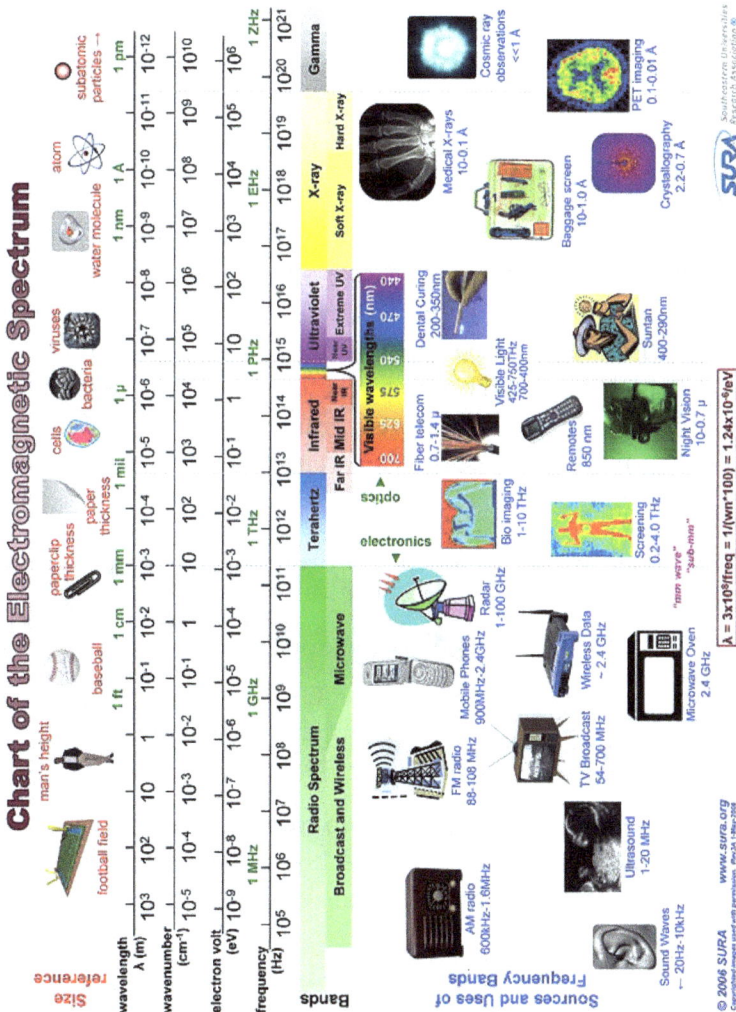

Chart of the Electromagnetic Spectrum

© 2006 SURA www.sura.org

vibrates at a certain frequency. The earth resonates at about 7.2 hertz – much the same as humans.[xviii/xix] Wikipedia has a good explanation of the Schumann Resonances which are global electromagnetic resonances, generated and excited by lightning discharges in the cavity formed by the earth's surface and the ionosphere.[xx]

Based on John's instructions, I created my own dowsing rods out of ¼-inch copper rods with ½-inch PVC pipes for handles (the copper rods need to move easily in the hands). I walked my apiary in a north to south direction and found the geomagnetic lines indeed were in front of and behind my hives. Walking in the east-west direction, I found the lines were on the sides of two hives together. The hives had been placed in the middle of the grid lines. I now dowse the locations of the geomagnetic lines whenever I need to locate a place to put my hives.

As serendipity will have it, it was right about this time I met Dr. Lee Barnes, a professional dowser with a Ph.D. in Environmental Horticulture. He is also an experienced naturalist and dedicated environmental activist. Lee combines his knowledge of natural forest communities, sustainable agriculture, and permaculture training with a bioregional focus and additional "awareness of place" using dowsing/biolocation techniques.

My hives in my main apiary had already been intuitively placed similar to the picture on the right. When I dowsed for the geo lines, I  found they were between the two rows of hives, between the hives, and between the outside hives and fence. There are three more hives on the other side of the enclosure.

John Harding considers the ideal geomagnetic field at these lines to resonate at between 190 and 250 hertz. Lee walked my property with his dowsing rods and located the same lines I found and more. He also found the one line running directly under my oldest hive going into its eighth year.

I have not seen Varroa in my hives except on very rare occasions. This was during my first and second year of beekeeping, and then they were on frames of large cell foundation and in a hive that was not in a geomagnetic grid. On one of those rare occasions, I watched one of my girls bite the legs off the Varroa and carry it out of the hive.

According to Resistant Bees: [xxi]

> "Dee Lusby discovered, after intensively studying beekeeping literature (from over 100 years and more), the cell size commonly used does not match the bees' needs."

Michael Bush's observation:

> *"Although I often see comb smaller than 4.9mm and sometimes larger than 4.9mm, 4.9mm has been sufficient to deal with Varroa issues in my experience. The bees seem more inclined to draw 4.9mm or smaller if the spacing in the brood nest is more natural, which I find to be 32mm (1-1/4"). This also lets less bees cover more brood to keep it warm which translates into a rapid buildup in the spring and less chilled brood. On natural comb, I see a 19-day development period as did the respected scientists, Francis Huber and Jan Dzierzon, when they were measuring it on natural comb. The shorter cycles reduce the average reproductive rate of a foundress Varroa mite from 1.5 +/- 0.5 down to 0.5 +/- 0.5.*

"On Apis cerana, the Varroa mite multiplies almost exclusively in the drone comb and on 'standard' foundation our worker cells are the same size as Apis cerana drone cells. I suspect that there are a lot less Varroa reproducing in the worker cells with smaller worker cells and more on the drones as they are in Apis cerana.

"The smaller the cell, the faster the gestation, the less Varroa offspring, and the less attractive the cell is to the Varroa. Apis cerana and Africanized bees build small cells and neither have big issues with Varroa.

Pre and Post Capping Times and Varroa

- *8 hours shorter capping time halves the number of Varroa infesting a brood cell.*

- *8 hours shorter post capping time halves the number of offspring of a Varroa in the brood cell.*

- *Accepted days for capping and post-capping, (based on observing bees on 5.4 mm comb)*

- *Capped 9 days after egg laid*

- *Emerges 21 days after egg laid*

Resistentbees.com is a website worth looking into as it provides more detailed information on raising resistant bees. I wish I had discovered this site in the beginning of my beekeeping career. They also commented:

"Another point is that small cell bees have a much longer life span, from 8 up to 12 weeks. The conventional large cell bees only have a lifespan of 6 weeks, which is considerably reduced by the use of chemicals, like anti Varroa treatments (Fernando

*Clatayud, biologist, Valencia, Spain). This longer
lifespan produces incredibly strong colonies as the work
inside of the colony can be done by a lot more bees,
which is a prerequisite for a healthy immune system.
Ongoing stress by the same amount of work to be done
by too few bees negatively affects the bee's immune
system.*

*"Dee Lusby found out that the cell size of 4.9mm is the
actual fundamental prerequisite in which the hygienic
behavior VSH appears, which means the active culling
of Varroa mites from the infected brood cells."*

I only assumed Varroa were in my hives. I rarely saw hive
beetles, but I wouldn't bother with them if I did. My original
hive survived eight years, and the daughter hives survived
seven, and six years, until all three froze during a freakish
winter storm. Because of their ages, I have often thought I was
a very successful beekeeper. After learning of the bees' ability
to detect electric impulses from flowers containing nectar, I
became convinced that there was far more information we
needed to understand about how honeybees work with
Mother.

To dowse your own
property, you can just use
plain copper wire bent at a
90° angle. Point the rods
parallel to the earth, straight
out in front of you. Walking
the property, take one slow step at a time. When you are over
a geomagnetic line, the rods will move to either cross each
other or point away from each other. Either way, the rods
show the direction of the geomagnetic line. Take another step
or two and the rods will straighten out and point forward
again away from you. Take another step, and you may find
another geomagnetic line. Use flags or stakes to mark the lines
as you go.

Lee also agreed that Ley lines are paths covering the earth's surface that could be seen but rarely understood. Scientists have learned that many holy sites are placed over where these geomagnetic lines cross.

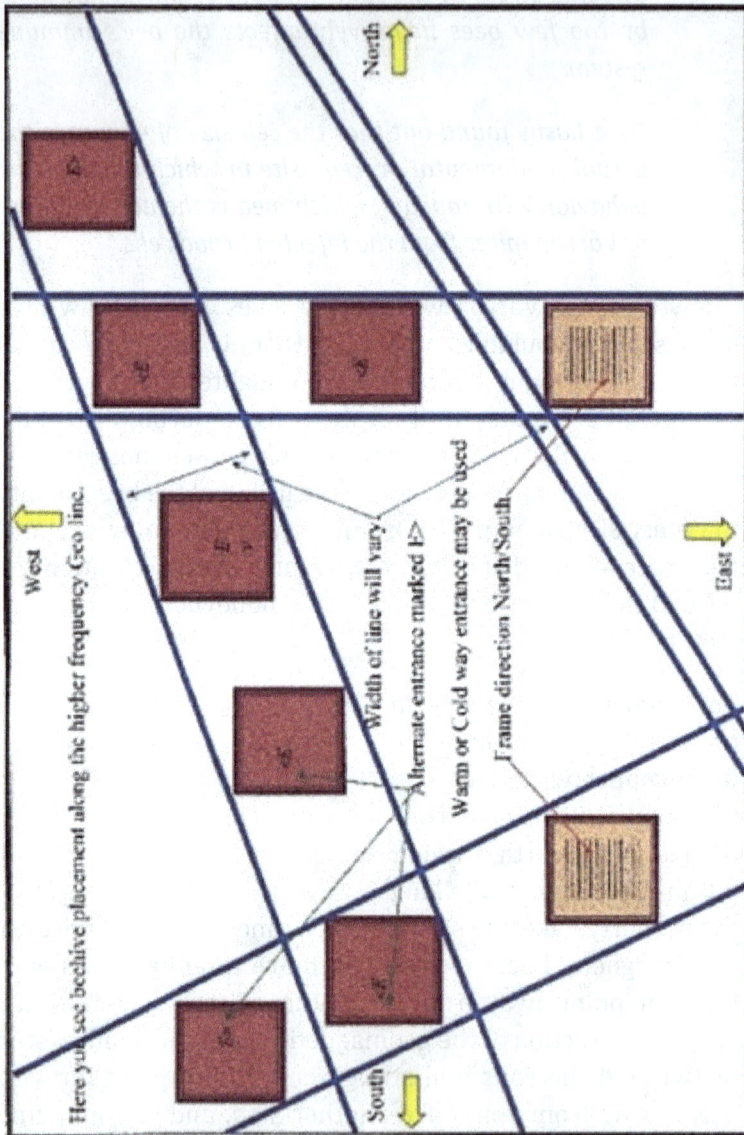

These lines are also called "geopathic lines" due to the contaminants in the water. Contaminants could be due to runoff from mines or caves, man altering the earth, chemicals from farm runoffs that seep into the earth, or something else. Feng Shui dictates that geopathic lines are harmful for humans and may cause illnesses.

Whether or not you believe in geomagnetic lines for pest control, I would suggest that you experiment and search for your own grid lines and set up two hives there. The Varroa is a mite, and mites do not like the high vibrations of 190 Hz to 250 Hz. You will find that not only does it work, but it will save you money, energy in dealing with Varroa and small hive beetles, and damage to your colony.

The Universe consists of a duality in which opposing sides will either balance each other out or give cause to resist each other. This duality is what keeps our world in balance, and Mother Nature will be in balance no matter what you do. The more you try to change her, the more aggressive she will be.

All animal species need time to evolve through their issues naturally. Pests in the beehive give bees a reason to fight for survival as in the Universal Law of Duality.[xxii] This Law also applies to the human immune system needing *Lactobacillus* and other good bacteria to fight the bad bacteria we continually give our digestive systems. A good immune system is needed to fight off illnesses. The less stressful a honeybees' life is the healthier it is and the more it can defend itself. The geomagnetic lines will go a long way to maintaining its health because the bee can better live in an environment that is compatible to their own vibrations, which is 190 to 250 hertz.

Placing Your Hives

I recommend laying down tar paper and nylon landscape fabric over it and around your hives. Your feet won't get tangled in weeds or grass and you will be able to see the dead bees under the hive entrance. It saves on weed eating near hives as well. When you do weed eat, the bees will come at you to investigate as they are curious animals; but they usually don't sting.

The picture above is what I did for Langstroth hives. Put down cement blocks under the 2x4 wooden frame at both ends and in the middle. Use a frame about four feet long for two hives or 8 feet long for four hives – both about 19-inches wide (this includes the 16x22-inch wide piece of plywood shelf placed on the frame between hives one and two and hives three and four). The frame should sit on the blocks without the blocks sticking out beyond the frame so that you won't trip.

If you have a solid bottom board under your hive bodies, use a level to set the frame to lean ¼ bubble, or ¼-inch, toward the front. This allows any moisture to flow out the entrance. If it is a screened bottom board, leveling the frame will be okay. I use cement blocks or treated lumber for hive placement and have found no issues with either. If you use a screened bottom board, set the hive so that air can get into the hive. A gap between the blocks will allow hive pests to fall through the screen. Without weeds to climb on, pests cannot climb back into the box.

Ideally, the hive is about 16 to 18 inches off the ground. This height usually discourages skunks and other similar sized animals from scratching at the entrance to eat bees. This puts the second-deep box at waist high for those of average height. An added medium super of honey is usually enough to get the colony through the winter.

The picture below is my Apiary 2. As you can see, you can build on a hill.

NOTE: The bees build honeycomb to the direction of the earth's core. So, if your hive is not leveled on all four sides, especially side to side, the comb will come out uneven in the frame and will make a mess when it is pulled out of the box.

Bees can count to three, recognize basic symbols, and see colors (with the exception of red which appears gray). If you have more than one hive and the hives are the same colors, you are apt to see what is called "drifting." That means the bees will go from one hive to another because they can't always distinguish which hive is theirs, especially if one hive is placed behind the other in the yard. If the hives have different colored boxes or designs painted on them (anything that will distinguish the difference), the drifting will stop. Bees cannot smell their queen's pheromone from 50 to 100 feet in the air.

Bees remember where their hive is. If you move a hive from one place in your apiary to another during the day, you will see them go back to the old site and regroup. It sometimes takes a little while for another bee from the new place to communicate to the others where the hive has been relocated. By nightfall, all bees are usually at the new site.

I have a solar-powered battery pack connected to the fence surrounding my apiary that helps to deter bears and other animals. The bees know that the space inside the fence is their territory and will usually not bother you while you are mowing or weed eating around the apiary.

After building my 80x80 square feet bee sanctuary, I moved my apiary. I built five topbar hives that hold about 28 Langstroth deep frames each. The inside hive boxes are set into a larger box with a two-inch air space between the inside and outside boxes. There is a small screened hole in the bottom that is covered in winter. The top lid has a stainless-steel piano hinge and a screened inner cover extending all the way across the 36-inch interior bee box. The inner screen is covered in November with a quilted pad to absorb the hive's condensation during winter time. I do this because I didn't like the black mold I found on the underside of the telescoping cover on other beehives. The pad absorbs the jove's condensation and keeps the bees warmer. Absorbing the hives excess condensation in the winter also helps prevent Chillbrood.

My main apiary (bee sanctuary) built in 2015.

5: Nuc/Package Care

Installing Packaged Bees

Packages will come in one, two, or three pounds. Three pounds is better for a strong colony. When it arrives, use a spray bottle containing one cup of water and one tablespoon of dissolved sugar or honey and lightly spritz the bees. They should settle down as they quench their thirst and get a little sugar for energy.

Take them out to the apiary where there is a permanent hive box already set up. The hive should contain eight or 10 frames, one with honey and pollen, if possible. Take off the telescoping lid and the inner cover and set them aside. Remove three frames from the center of your hive box. Using a knife or screwdriver, remove the can of sugar feed from the circle in the top of the wooden package. The queen cage will be hanging on the inside and attached to a nylon strip stapled to the outside of the box. Use a screwdriver to remove the staple while holding on to the nylon strip. Gently set the queen cage aside in the shade, protecting the queen from the sun.

Gently shake the bees out of the wooden package into the hive box. It's okay to tap the sides of the package. It is almost impossible to get all the bees out, so set the package box down on the ground in front of the entrance. Any remaining bees will make it into the hive. Carefully place the three frames back into the hive. In the very center place the queen cage between two frames with the solid bottom facing up and close the frames on either side to hold the queen cage. The nurse bees will eat the white fondant candy shoved into a hole at the end of the queen cage to let her out. Square off the corners by using the curved end of your hive tool and twist it to put equal distance between the outside frames and side walls. You will need to feed your packaged bees unless you are able to put in a couple of frames of honey and pollen.

Queens in packages are not usually raised by the bees that came with the package; but are raised outside of the hive then placed in queen cages with a few extra nurse bees. By the time the queen is released from her cage, at least 24 hours or more, enough time has passed for her pheromones to be passed around the small colony to calm the bees.

The next day, check the hive to make sure the queen has been released. If not, use a knife to remove the cork on one end of the queen cage. Leave the cage in the hive for one more day. Remove the empty queen cage the next day after all bees have left the cage. Be sure to square off the frames.

Installing Your Nuc of Bees

After 24 hours, set your nuc alongside of its permanent hive. Open the top and inner lid of your hive body and the lid of your nuc. Place two frames next to the west side in the hive box first if it is an 8-frame Langstroth hive or three frames if it is a 10-frame hive. If possible, place at least one full frame of honey next to the west wall of the box. Honey placed next to the outside wall helps to insulate the hive against the western sun. Place one frame to the eastern wall if it is an 8-frame or two if it is a 10-frame hive.

In the nuc box, use the curved end of your hive tool and gently twist the tool at both ends of the frame next to the left wall to move the frames apart. If you use the flat end, you often end up damaging the comb and this excites the bees. I use the frame gripper with the wide grips rather than the one with pointed ends. The pointed ends often slip into the comb, tearing it, and you don't have a good grip on the frame. The nuc box is tight, so it is wise to slowly lift frames straight up and out of the nuc box so that you don't damage the queen.

Examine the frame to see if you can see the queen. Slowly place the examined frame next to the frame on the left already in the hive box and gently push it to touch the other frame. Separate the second frame in the nuc, pick it straight up, examine it, and place it next to the one you just put in the hive box. Every frame is taken out of the nuc box and placed in the same position in the hive box. As you examine each frame for the queen and any anomalies, start getting used to looking at everything. As you put each frame from the nuc into the permanent hive, push them close together as you continue until you place all five frames from the nuc box in the permanent hive box.

Twist the rounded end of your hive tool in the inside corners of the hive box to square off the corners of the frames to put equal distance from the frames and inside edge of the box. This will put about a 5/8-inch space between the side walls and frames. This also helps to teach the bees not to build the wax out wider between the frames which can be a mess when pulling the frames apart again. Bees are like animals, and you can train them to a small degree. If there are any bees in the nuc, shake them out into the hive. If there are bees left in the box, leave it standing at an angle below the hive entrance. By evening, the box will be empty and all the bees will be in their permanent home.

Next, put on the inner screen cover by slowly lowering it onto the hive box in a circular motion. The bees will move out of the way. Any openings on the side of the inner screen cover should be facing up to allow the bees to leave should they get caught above the screen cover. Lower the top telescoping cover as you did the inner cover. Tell your bees you're leaving. Once you've gently left, leave your nuc box until evening. When you go back to get it, remove it from under the hive entrance, clean it, and save it for when you make your own split.

On occasion, depending on when the hive was put together, you may find queen cells. This usually means the queen was killed, and the bees have decided to make their own queen. This is called supersede. The nuc provider will often raise queens separately and place them inside a nuc. I have found many of my packaged bees will allow the queen to lay enough eggs for the workers to raise several queens. This taught me that colonies prefer to raise their own queens.

Splitting a Full Hive

If you are one of the lucky ones with a very strong colony, you may have the opportunity of making a split during your first season. I don't recommend making a split after July 1st as you would be approaching the dearth period, a time when there is usually nothing to harvest and you'll end up having to feed your bees.

Only about 20 percent of swarms survive, so I usually split my colonies in mid-spring before they get the notion to swarm. You will need to split the colony into a 5-frame nuc if, in an 8-frame, 2-deep, Langstroth hive, you have 16 frames and 12-14 are filled with brood and stores. There are some who will split earlier or make two colonies with just two or three frames in each nuc. I prefer to have two very strong colonies, rather than three or four weak ones. My nucs will have no less than four frames full of brood, eggs, larvae, and nurse bees with extra forage bees shaken in.

Add a frame with honeycomb or empty. But I would prefer to add one frame of honey, with pollen if possible, as there are more nurse bees than there are foragers. The honey will feed the larvae until they are capped and the nurse bees until they evolve into foragers. The pollen has honey added to make the beebread, which is their protein. By the time the brood has hatched and the honey is gone, the queen is laying eggs in the spaces where there was honey and the nurse bees have evolved into foragers. Starting out a nuc this way makes for a healthy, strong colony.

After I make the nuc, I take it up the road about five miles away so that the queen will mate with drones outside of her permanent domain area. You will hope your queen is a *hussy* and mates with at least 12 to 20 drones.

Bees like to forage about a quarter mile from their hive but will travel up to two miles or more for food. After two miles, their stores will probably be gone before they get back to the hive. Queens and drones will travel up to five miles to mate.

Drones carry the genetic markers, and different drones carrying different markers will make a diverse colony. The more diverse the genetics, the healthier, more intelligent, and more hygienic your colony will be. Different drones are the reasons you will find different colored and different sized bees in your hive. A watered-down gene pool weakens the colonies and causes one of our biggest problems with Colony Collapse Disorder (CCD). Look at feral colonies and ask yourself why they survive over domesticated colonies. The queens from feral colonies don't selectively choose their mates as in the cases of artificially inseminated or managed queens in mating yards.

I usually wait at least 14 to16 days after relocating the nuc before looking into it. Checking too early, you risk tearing queen cells because the spacing in the nuc box is tight. This is also another reason to learn to bring your frames straight up and out of the hive rather than at an angle.

I can recall a time when it rained hard for 29 solid days straight, not just a drizzle. Before the rainfall, I had made a split and anticipated a queen. When I was finally able to check the nuc after the rainfall, there was no queen. Beekeepers have told me that a queen should mate within 14 days or she may be lost. Intuition told me to wait. She finally started laying eggs a few days later. I also learned that the Caucasian bee will not lay eggs unless there is enough food available. There wasn't any in the nuc. After that, I made sure I had honey and beebread in the hive with all the splits. Every little bit of knowledge you gain helps you in the overall picture.

When a queen hatches during the day, she will need another 24 hours to "harden" – her exoskeleton will get hard. A new virgin queen looks very similar to a worker and usually isn't easily spotted until after she has mated and her abdomen swells larger, giving her that awkward walk. This takes about three days. The fatter your queen's abdomen is, the healthier she will be. The time it takes after the new queen hatches until she starts laying eggs can be as long as a few weeks. You need to be patient.

As soon as the new queen is laying eggs, close up the nuc's entrance after dark or very early in the morning and take it back to its permanent location. Open the entrance and wait 24 hours before putting it into its permanent home. Remember, moving the bees traumatizes them, so allow them the time to calm down. When you open the entrance and they come out, watch them take their orientation flights. They don't go anywhere. They just fly around in circles to get a sense of where they are in relation to the sun.

Observing Your Swarms

If you don't know the genetics or from where the swarm came, you may not want to take just any swarms offered to you because you don't want your apiary infested with hybrid or sick bees. I also don't want a swarm infested with Varroa. When a colony is unhappy, for whatever reason, they will leave.

Just to share a personal story, my first swarm came from my first hive. It was a Laurel and Hardy comedy routine as I climbed the 12-foot ladder and used a 10 foot, one-inch PVC pipe with a bee brush taped to one end. I brushed a few bees, lowered the pipe, and shook the bees into the nuc box. After half the swarm was in the box, I was proud of myself but found the process dangerous because I am afraid of heights and had no idea of what I was doing. An hour later, the swarm was back in the tree.

I then remembered a trick a veteran beekeeper shared with me. He starts his weed eater without the string running; puts it close to the swarm; and points the weed eater to the box. He does this about three times before they go into their new home. So, I used the PVC pipe to gently tap on the tree branch then tapped the box. I did this about three times. It was exciting to watch the bees go down to the nuc box in a thick stream, land on the ground, and march in. Bees are just as curious as we are. It took about 20 minutes for the swarm to enter their nuc hive. I was totally amazed that it worked. That evening, I placed the nuc in its permanent place in the apiary and into its permanent hive box a couple weeks later. This was before I learned about moving the nuc to a new location.

Raising Queens

Before swarming, the old queen will lay less eggs, but enough eggs to assure that the colony will have a new queen. More often than not, I have had packages supersede within a month after allowing the old queen to lay enough eggs. Because I respect the hive's choice, I do not pinch off the extra queen cells the workers raise after making a split. Only the bees (not beekeepers) know which queen out of the half dozen or more queen cells is going to be the strongest.

In the hive, it takes a lot of bee pollen to produce royal jelly. If there isn't enough bee pollen, there won't be enough quality royal jelly to feed the queen. Please note: royal jelly is *not* what makes a queen.[xxiii]

> "Beebread and honey are derived from plant materials, and like many plant materials, they contain a variety of phenolic chemicals. We eat them all the time; flavonoids are the plant chemicals that give plants their unique flavors (and help plants discourage plant-eating insects, among other functions).
>
> Royal jelly, however, has no detectable phenolic acids. None. From previous research, the researchers knew that flavonoids increase immune responses of adult worker bees. That's a good thing; it has the side effect of helping bees detoxify pesticides faster."

The bees like to use a three to four-day old larvae (this includes the egg stage) for their queens. The first queen out will go around to all the other queen cells, put a hole in the side of the cells, and sting the queens to death. The workers then remove the dead queen larvae and break down the queen cells, usually in about 24 hours.

My queens are raised in the splits. I don't pinch queens off the combs nor do I sell the queen cells or hatched queens.

6: Hive Inspection

The primary premise behind BEe Perspective Beekeeping is keeping your bees out of stress. Their immune system is 67 percent optimal. Anytime you go into the hive, you set them back a day. Any herbicide spraying that is done around them (either next to them or within ¼ mile) stresses them. Unfortunately, stress can cause European Foulbrood (EFB) disease. The less often you enter the hive, the healthier your bees will be, especially during the spring, which is their busiest season. I do suggest you inspect them at least once a week in the spring, twice a month in summer, and monthly thereafter until the temperature goes below 60°F. Afterwards, you should only need to lift the lid to smell the hive or lift the hive body to determine the weight of the hive.

Approaching Your Hives

When you approach your bees, speak or chant to let them know it is you. You should do this every time you approach their hive. They will remember your voice, and it helps to calm them. They will also recognize your face.

When a hive is busy collecting nectar and pollen sometime around mid-March to May, they will often have a low hum sound. This is the sound of contentment. If you close your eyes and listen carefully, the hum can be heard as a monotone sound. If the bees are annoyed or angry, their sound will increase to a higher pitch and often with different tones. Smoking the bees interferes with this form of communication.

In the 1950s, Eddie Woods, a British Broadcasting Corporation (BBC) sound engineer, created an ApiDictor, which is a device that can record honeybee sounds in the hive. He discovered that wings vibrate anywhere from 190 to 250 hertz for different tasks. The vibrations increase to 300 hertz for swarms. My one swarm sounded like a tornado or a train when it left the hive.

A hertz is the number of cycles in a sound wave. Middle C, which is about 261 hertz. A carpenter bee will unleash the pollen when it vibrates its wings to the key of C.[xxiv] Carl Zimmer, a *New York Times* journalist, published the following in July 2013 about how a bumblebee releases pollen:[xxv]

> *"Only bumblebees and certain other insects can get this pollen out. In every case, the method is the same: the pollinator grabs the tube with its jaws and starts vibrating hundreds of times a second .... It has to hold on, because the vibrations are so strong that otherwise it could come flying off the flower."*

I always advocate listening to your bees before approaching the hive, while opening and closing the top cover, and during inspections. The hive's sounds indicate what is actually going on in the hive. Vibrational sounds can indicate when a swarm will happen several days before the fact. It takes a few years and comparing a lot of hives to understand this form of communication. Chances are you are intuitive enough to sense the sounds if you can listen carefully.

As you approach the hive:

1. Listen to the sounds of your bees. Look at the entrance. Based on the time of the year, check the following:

   a. How much activity is there at the entrance? There should be a lot during spring and summer. If not, something may be wrong. There will be less activity going into fall because of less drones.

   b. See how many bees are on the ground. There will always be a few throughout the season and a lot in the fall when drones are kicked out. But you need to inspect the hive if there are a lot on the ground in the spring or summer. Look for the following:

      i. Are there any with crippled wings?

      ii. Are the bees crawling on the ground?

      iii. Do they have short abdomens?

   c. If you see any bees under, to the side, or to the back of the hive, you probably have robber bees looking to steal honey. Your hive entrance will then need to be taken down to about ¾-inch, especially during the dearth. During the honey flow, I leave the entrances wide open.

Inspecting a Langstroth Hive

Most beekeepers use a smoker to calm their bees. When a hive is opened, the bees immediately put out the attack pheromone. Smoking masks the attack pheromone; after about 20 seconds, the bees may calm down.[xxvi] I don't smoke my bees. My concern is the smoke interfering with the communication pheromones in the hive. The bees have to work all the harder to spread the pheromones after you close up. The smoke also gets on the wax, in the honey, the bees, everything – all of it causing stress.

On occasion, I found that a homemade solution of one tablespoon of sugar or honey to one cup of water or more in a spray bottle works well when spritzing them very lightly. The bees will go to the task of grooming each other. If you should use this method, be sure to rinse the tip of the bottle once you've finished spritzing. Otherwise, the sugar dries and clogs your sprayer.

NOTE: Sometimes you come across an "ornery" hive. This is a hive that stings without provocation and the sound of their buzzing is really loud and angry after you open the hive. When I have had bees with African traits, they will sound angry and loud and will sting at every opportunity. Other beekeepers may pinch the queen and let the hive supersede or put in another queen. Smoke or sugar water may help those bees. I try not to take those kinds of bees into my apiary.

You never work from in front of the hive because you will block the entrance. Step behind the hive, tap twice on the side then gently lift the lid just enough for you to take a deep breath. If it smells of warm honey, you probably won't need to go into the hive. However, you should go into your hives at least twice a month during late spring and summer to keep the frames clean and to check that you still have a queen.

Keeping notes may be a great help in understanding how your beehives expanded and why they didn't. It will also give you a visual for when you think you may need to add more equipment or make a split. You may want to record the percentages for nectar, honey, brood, and beebread; empty frames; and queen cells and queen cups. You may want to use a tape recorder or your cell phone while doing your inspections. Cell phones need to be kept off the hot surfaces like the top cover if it is made of metal. They tend to shut off when they get too hot from the heat radiating off the metal. I use the following abbreviations when transcribing:

- Nectar - N
- Honey - H
- Brood - B
- Larva - L
- Beebread - BB
- Empty Frame - MT
- Queen Cell - QC
- Queen Cup - CUP

The difference between queen cell and queen cup is that the queen cell has a larva in it. Bees always have extra cups on a few frames for emergencies.

You may also want to note at the beginning of each inspection the weather conditions, wind speed, and temperature. Also note whether it is sunny or cloudy, if there is a drought, what plants are growing, the pollen color, and more. This may give you an idea of what to expect in certain situations. Also, the first time you do an inspection, record the number or name of your hive. Note the source from where the bees came, and the date you put it into its permanent home. Putting down the color of the hive also helps to keep the image straight in your head when going back over your notes.

Keeping detailed notes will give you the following:

- A visual record of the seasonal changes and how your bees behaved. What was blooming and for how long? Did it rain too much? What was the weather and how much did it affect the hive?

- How long was the dearth? When did it start? When did it stop? Did you even have a dearth?

- How fast did the hive build up?

- Did the hive supersede. When and why?

- The kind of personality the colony has: how gentle it is, how much honey did it produce, and how much pollen and propolis did it store? Is the colony gentle?

- Does the hive have enough honey or beebread for winter?

- What kind of brood pattern that would indicate whether or not you may need to requeen? How active was the queen in laying eggs? Was she slow? Are there too many holes between capped brood?

- The number of drones (were there more than usual? Less than usual?) In the spring, there should be drones laid in the bottom corners of several frames. Where they were laid should be noted as well. Sometimes they are mostly laid in one frame. Some hives follow their own ideas and not what is written in the books or what other beekeepers tell you.

- When you should make a split.

- Did the hive swarm? Frequent inspections will show you the number of bees you have while they expanded their colony and how small the colony is after they have swarmed.

- Do you see Varroa or Small Hive Beetles? If not, your hive is probably resistant and hygienic in getting rid of the pests.

It may seem like a lot of trouble, but you can get a pretty good detailed image of what you might expect from each colony and the hive's personality. Its personality is based on what kind of and how many drones had mated with the queen. You can determine where you place your splits based on how strong the colony is. The inspections gave me an idea of what to expect from each year.

WEAR APPROPRIATE CLOTHING

No matter how gentle you are, you may still want to wear a jacket and veil. There's nothing like getting stung by many bees when you drop a frame. Bees like to sting on the warm parts of the body as they know this is where it is the most sensitive and will be more painful. Also, you don't want them stinging around your eyes. And, frankly, I don't want to be so arrogant that I kill my bees. When I put my first nuc in its permanent hive, I was very arrogant in thinking I love my bees so why would they sting me. I didn't count on dropping a frame and being stung 40 times.

MOVE RESPECTIVELY

If you move slowly with no loud noises or fast movements, your bees will usually work with you. Of course, this depends on your bee species. Africanized bees can be just plain ornery no matter how nice you are and will sting any way. Work in a continual motion when separating, lifting, inspecting, and putting the frames back into the hive. Moving tools from one hand to another over the open hive can excite the bees. Learn to use both hands when working with tools.

RAISE THE TELESCOPING LID AND SMELL

Slowly raise the telescoping lid and inhale deeply. If it smells like warm honey, you may not need to go any further unless it has been more than two weeks since your last inspection and it's still early in the season. If you smell something rotting or see many pests or dead bees, you will definitely need to go in and determine what is going on. Something rotting is either going to be European Foulbrood (EFB), American Foulbrood (AFB), or Idiopathic Brood Disease (IBDS). These are covered later on in the disease section of the book. Intuition or sight will tell you if you have a lot of pests, which will indicate a weak hive.

Carefully and slowly take the lid off. Check to see if there is any condensation on the top lid. Condensation indicates the moisture is not leaving the hive. At certain times of the year, your bees could develop chill brood (discussed in disease section). Lift the front of the lid up and away from your face and set the lid to the side, topside down and preferably on a shelf next to the hive.

If the lid is stuck, put the flat part of your hive tool between the cover and hive box and pull up on the hive tool. If you hear a cracking noise when separating equipment, stop and count to 30 seconds if this is your first time, 10 seconds if you have been in the hive before. This will give the bees time to calm down. Do this every time you hear noises in separating any piece of equipment during an inspection. Bees don't like surprises.

I never stay in the hive longer than 30 minutes, and then only if the temperature is in the mid-70s or hotter. It takes a lot of work for the bees to keep the hive at about 95°F. In my agricultural zone 6/7 area, I check my hives on days when the temperature is above 60°F. Mid-March to the first of April is usually warm enough for me to stay in the hive a little longer.

GET OUT WHEN BEES ARE EXCITED

If you have honeybees that are usually calm and they get excited while you are inspecting them, you need to get out. Don't take it personal. Bees are sensitive to air pressure and know when it is going to rain, even when you see clear skies. They don't like their roof opened if there is a chance of rain (no more than you would appreciate someone opening your house roof). There may also be something else going on in the hive to which you have not been invited (i.e., their queen has hatched; the queen is being prepped for or has returned from mating; or there are other private matters going on). You also may have also been in the hive too long or have killed too many bees or the queen. To repeat: keeping the bees out of stress is your number one goal.

Remember that every time you go into a hive, no matter how short or long a time you were in it, you set the colony back one whole day. That is how much stress you create when you enter a beehive and how long it may take them to bring the hive temperature back up. Be sure to watch their flying patterns and listen to the vibrational sounds of their wings, as this is how they communicate with you. The sound of a gentle hive being content with you will sound harmonious. The vibrational sounds of an agitated hive will sound loud and the bees will fly all over the place, especially around your head. Always stay focused when you are in your hive. The bees know when your mind is elsewhere and will either tap your veil, your head, or sting you to get you focused.

Go Into the Hive

Take off the inner screened cover. I used to use a solid cover with an oval hole in winter. I didn't like the mold on the solid inner cover, so now I use an inner screened cover on all my hives but I place a pad over the inner cover during winter to collect the condensation the bees emit. Place the inner cover, right side up on the telescoping cover, angled where its four corners are touching each side of the top cover. On hot days, this will prevent the sides of each hive component from sticking together because of the propolis on the top edges of the boxes. Also, you won't kill as many bees if you don't stack the equipment precisely on top of each other.

NOTE: If you want to smoke, have a mentor show how to start a smoker. You can also find instructions on YouTube on the internet. If you do smoke, be sure that the smoke is cool to your hands. Hot smoke will burn your bees, especially their wings. Puff a couple of short puffs at the entrance. You may want to puff a couple of times over the bees when you open the hive.

Place the honey super, usually a medium or a deep, with the four corners resting on each side of the inner cover. This is where you need to establish a rote system. This is doing your inspection precisely the same way each time you inspect when moving, placing your frames, using both hands to hold your tools, etc. A rote system will allow the bees to memorize it and work with you. As before, go slowly without fast or jerky movements and no loud noises. Continue to talk softly to your bees. They will recognize your voice. If you are afraid, you will emit a pheromone they can smell as fear and most likely will sting you (much like a dog would bite when it smells fear).

If you have a 2-box brood system, take the next box off and place it angled on the previous box. The idea is to get to the bottom box. The queen moves swiftly and hides. She will keep going down to the bottom box. Inspecting each box before putting it back will better help you to find the queen.

MAKE THE ACTUAL INSPECTION

Place your frame perch on the unobstructed side of the box you are going to inspect which should be sitting on the bottom board.

If there is wax (burr comb) between the frames, use the flat end of your hive tool and cut the wax down the center of the two frames. This will prevent you from tugging or pulling on the frame and tearing the wax. The frame may also be attached to the frame in the box below. This will happen if your boxes do not have the 3/8-inch bee space between the boxes, if it has been a long time since your last inspection, or if your bees just plainly needed to use wax. This is another reason to work with one frame at a time.

Use the curved end of your hive tool by placing it between the frames at both ends and twist the tool to loosen it off the end shelf of the box and to separate the frames. The bees propolize everything. To get the bees out of the way, use the frame grip to place it in the center of the frame top and slowly move it back and forth across the frame as you slowly close the frame grip. Pick the frame up in a slow, straight up motion. Pulling the frame up at an angle risks you tearing the queen cell, should there be a one on the frame.

With a firm hold on the frame grip, turn the frame so that you can look at both sides. Do not hold the frame upside down. Wax is built at a 9-degree angle; if you turn the frame upside down, the nectar will flow out and the bees get angry. You will need to hold the frame in your hands if you have to clean it. When finished cleaning the frame, place it on the frame perch and move the frame close to the box to give room for more frames.

If this is a honey super and you still want to inspect it, you can place three or four frames on the frame perch. If it is the brood box, you should place no more than two frames on the perch as the first one or two frames are either empty or filled with beebread and/or honey. If there is brood on the frame and you have not spotted the queen, do not place the frame on the perch. You don't want to risk dropping the queen outside the box. Keep the frame over the box as you inspect it. During an inspection with a group of people, I watched the queen on the frame I was inspecting fly over to a hive being inspected behind me. All of us watched my queen kill the queen in the other hive. No one knew why she flew out of her original hive.

Once the first two frames are on the frame perch, inspect the third frame and move it to the empty space next to the wall. Finish inspecting each frame, pushing them together as you go, and recording your notes. Go through each frame to check for any anomalies, cleaning the frames as you go. Keep a container nearby for your scrapings. Dropping them on the ground only makes for dirty tracks into the house.

INSPECT FRAMES

1. The bees will burr up (putting wax between frames, on top, and on the bottom, wherever they have room) that is larger than the sacred 3/8-inch bee space. Being an animal, you can train the bee to a degree. If you take the time to gently scrape the frames with the curved end of your hive tool and the flat end to scrape the insides of the box each and every time, they will cut back on the burring. If there is a 3/8-inch bee space

between the frames and between the boxes, they will usually have a neater hive. Also, clean the frame shelves of the boxes. DO NOT SCRAPE THE PROPOLIS OFF THE EDGES OF THE BOXES. THIS PROPOLIS PROTECTS THE BEES FROM DISEASES. A VERY THIN COAT OF PROPOLIS IS WHAT THE BEES LINE THE CELLS WITH AFTER EACH TIME A BEE HATCHES. THEY DON'T REMOVE ANYTHING OR CLEAN THE CELLS. PROPOLIS IS OBTAINED FROM THE RESINS OF TREES AND PLANTS AND IS ANTI-MICROBIAL, ANTI-BACTERIAL, ANTI-VIRAL AND ANTI-FUNGAL.

2. If you inspect regularly (every week or so during the busy seasons) and you see the queen in the bottom box, you shouldn't have to do much. Just put the hive back together, giving the top box a quick glance at a few frames in the center to determine the quality of the queen's laying pattern.

3. The queen's laying pattern will change with the seasons. Brood will fill the frame in the early spring. As the season heats up, there will be more empty cells throughout the brood nest, which assure good temperature control. However, if you see too many empty cells in early to mid-spring, your queen probably needs replacing. If you know for a fact that she does need replacing, be sure there are a lot of eggs and young larvae on at least two frames. Eggs stand up in the cell. If the larvae are lying down on the rhomboid, the egg has hatched. If you feel you have enough eggs and larvae, crush the queen, and the hive will make another. My suggestion is to check with an experienced beekeeper.

4. If you decide to go into the top box, inspect it while it sits to the side without putting it back on the bottom box you just inspected. The queen moves quickly out of sunlight and out of your way. The queen has nowhere to go. If you don't see her in the bottom box,

inspecting the top box while it is on the inner cover will give you a better chance of finding her. If not, you can go back to the bottom box.

5. IMPORTANT NOTE: When putting the hive back together, don't fear of putting the boxes together because of how many bees there are on the edges of the box. The bees may be festooning (holding onto each other like a clustered ladder) below the frames so, using the hand-holds on the sides of the box, lift one box up and hover over the box below. Hold the right side of the box up at an angle and place the left side on the box below. Slowly slide the box around, while still holding the right side at an angle, until the back and front corners are on the left are aligned with the bottom box. Gently and slowly lower the box with soft, short bounces until it gradually touches the other three edges down on the bottom box. Gently bouncing the box gives the bees time to move out of the way. Very few bees die using this method, and there is far less aggravation because of dead bees. The bees know you mean no harm when you are gentle.

6. Pick up the inner cover and in a small, slow, circular motion, lower the cover down onto the top of the hive box. Bees sometimes get caught between the inner and top covers trying to get back into the hive. The holes on the sides of the inner cover face up and allow the bees to escape.

7. Place the top cover the same way as you did with the inner cover. Once it is down on the inner cover, push the top lid to the front of the hive. This allows better air flow, and any bees caught on top of the inner cover will have room to escape. It also acts like an overhang for the porch at the entrance.

PUT THE FRAMES BACK TOGETHER

Bees are very organized and very particular about how they set up their house. When putting the frames back into the box, put them back in the exact same position and order from which you took them. I make sure that new frames with the foundation strips in the top of the frame are in the Housel Position when going into the hive. Otherwise, the frames go back exactly the way they came out. Most beekeepers just put frames in the hive however they can. So, even if the frames are not in the Housel Position, the bees will have the hive organized.

BROOD PATTERN

The day after Solstice, the queen will usually start laying her eggs in a Langstroth hive in the center of the hive in a small sun-wise circle in the center of a frame. She will lay eggs on the other side of the frame in the same way. She then will lay eggs in frames on either side of the center frames and work toward the walls. She will go back and forth on each frame increasing the laying pattern.

It may be one to two weeks, sometimes sooner if it is a nuc, for your colony to fill a deep brood box. When the one box is filled with brood and stores with only one to two empty frames remaining, put on another deep box filled with frames of 4.9mm cell strips placed in the top of the frames. Often, you can put in frames with the strips at the top of every other frame. Your bees may fill these frames with nectar, pollen, and beebread, and perhaps more brood. Later in the season, they usually don't lay brood for the sake of increasing the colony, but lay in as much food as possible, especially during the fall harvest.

If the queen continues to lay brood to within two empty frames, you will need to either split the colony (depending on the time of year) or add a medium or deep box which they will fill with food and use for the coming winter. If you wait until the first box is totally full, the bees will get the notion to swarm. Adding the extra boxes will give them more room and usually prevents swarming. It is said that the queen will not lay above 18", which is about two deeps or three medium boxes.

Depending on when you get your nuc or package, it is not uncommon to have just one box of brood during the first winter. The bees will always have honey at the top (ceiling) of the frames. It will either be only at the top of each frame if there is only one box with possibly a frame of honey next to the walls, or the honey will be in the top box with the brood nest in the bottom box. If the bees are not increasing the colony fast enough by July, think before adding another box. And too much space, too soon, will overwhelm the bees. I have had colonies survive the winter with only one deep box.

The first year of beekeeping is a challenge because you will need to get used to the hive equipment; start overcoming the intimidation of 50,000+ bees; start learning how to communicate with the bees; and learning each hive's personality. By the end of the first year, you should have established a rote system for inspection – a point where you don't have to think about what you're doing with the equipment as you go through the hive. It is also the year of learning what to look for in your hive. Your abilities to detect diseases and causes are usually learned by the end of the second or third year. The communication part may be soon, later, or not at all.

Brood pattern may also differ each year. The norm is having honey at the top of the frame formed in an arc. Below the honey, stored pollen and beebread may take up about half an inch. Sometimes drone cells will be next, and then the worker brood will follow all the way down to the bottom. Drones may also be at the bottom corners in a triangular pattern, along with more pollen and nectar. This will most often be in a one-brood-box hive. In a two-deep hive, the brood may all be on the bottom box all across the frame with the drones on a couple of frames near the outside wall. I have seen brood in the front half of the frame and stores in the back half of the frame. Everything depends on your bees; your hive setup; the age of the hive; and the hive's personality. It may also be that the geomagnetic lines may have changed their energy frequencies and the bees have changed with them.

The second year will make for a stronger colony and easier to make splits with two deeps. After locating the queen in one deep box, I would keep it with old hive equipment and leave her in the old apiary. The other deep brood box would be placed on a bottom board with an added inner and top cover to complete the hive body then moved it to another location.

If obtained in the spring, a good beehive colony going into the winter will consist of one to two deep boxes and at least one full medium box of honey containing at least one frame of beebread.

Remember, bees are notional. You won't usually make a split the first year. It has been my experience that if your bees have Africanized genes, they will usually show the following four traits:

1. They swarm often, up to 11 to 13 times a year.

2. They are stingy with the honey and store only what they need.

3. They are very aggressive and will chase you outside of the vicinity of the apiary and sting you without provocation.

4. They will fly at the lowest temperatures but can only take extreme cold for about three days before dying.

7: Communicate with Your Bees

The first year of beekeeping is spent getting used to your hive's personality. Each species of bees has their own way of doing things. Of the three castes in the hive, the drone is the caste that carries the genetic markers of the honeybee. When your queen mates from different drones, you are going to get different colored bees and different sized bees within the hive. Each hive will have different personalities based on the queen and the different drones.

Learn Different Colony Castes

On the next page is a picture of three colony castes [xxvii] that live in a hive with their ages from egg to hatching. The first three days, the egg stage, is when the egg stands up in the cell. The fourth day, the egg hatches and lies down to begin the larval stage. The larval stage is only five days. This can be confusing because you will hear others talk about "the eighth day of larva." On the eighth day, the cell is filled with honey and then capped, unless it is 4.9mm in which case it may be capped on the seventh day. Days 9 through 11 are the prepupa stage or the time when the bee starts its metamorphoses from a larva into an adult bee. The pupa stage is when the bee finishes developing (12 to 16 days for the queen, 12 to 21 days for the worker, and 12 to 24 days for the drone). All larvae are given royal jelly during the first three days of the egg stage. Once the worker and drone become larvae, they are fed worker jelly containing honey and beebread.

The queen is the only caste that is fed royal jelly throughout her life from egg to hatching to death. Sugar is another important factor that may influence caste determination. Asencot and Lensky found that the food of 1-to 3-day old queen larvae contained 12.4 percent sugars, which was approximately four times of that found in worker jelly.[xxviii] Because I don't know which larva among the numerous queen cells has the strongest or weakest queen, I leave the extra cells on the frame in a hive that is making their own queen. This is also why I don't introduce queens from another source. I don't know if it is a weak or strong queen.

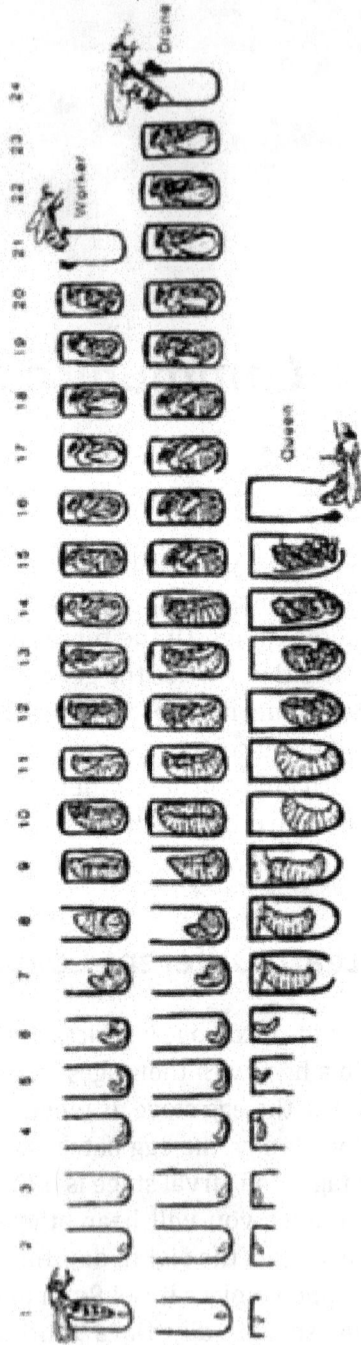

It is important to memorize the information in the cast chart as it will come in handy for other apiary projects. You will also have a better picture of other things going on in the hive than just queen rearing. Knowing the stages of the honeybee from egg to hatching will help you to know when to use Apilarnil, a hive larvae product that is used in apitherapy.

Listen to Your Bees

When you approach your hive, listen to the sounds. Is the sound uniform? Does it sound scattered like a lot of bees making their individual sounds? Close your eyes. When a hive is happy the bees buzzing sounds are together enough that the sound will be a low, soft humming, and almost a monotone quality. This will take a practiced ear and may sometimes take a couple years. Note that if your beehives are placed tightly close together in the apiary within a very small space, it will be more difficult to communicate with them. The bees need space to move around outside and to communicate with those of their own hive. The bee colonies do not like to live with other colonies in trees, houses, etc.

Listen to your bees and watch them move in front of their hives. Does there seem to be a lot of noise going on inside? Listen while they harvest during a honey flow and listen while they multiply their brood. Hum or sing softly to them and listen to them communicate with you. Watch their movements when you are in the hive, and chuckle as they watch you from between the frames. Watch them waggle their butts at you. I cannot explain this communication any clearer because there are few words to describe this part of beekeeping. It needs to be experienced.

If you open your bees' hive, and the bees come out and scatter chaotically in different directions with different bee sounds, the hive may be queenless. I remember a hive that I went into after a two-week period. They acted normal in sound, and movement. They were even bringing in nectar and pollen. Going through the hive I learned there wasn't a queen. It took three tries to get them to make a queen from an inserted frame from another hive. I was also surprised at not finding a laying worker. So sometimes the bees will sound like their colony is *queenright*, meaning there is a queen, even when there is none to be found.

If the sounds of your bees increase after opening the hive and the sound lasts longer than a few minutes, they are usually agitated for one of the following reasons:

- **They know it's going to rain; they can feel the barometric pressure in the air.** While it may seem sunny to you, your bees know it will rain in just a few hours. Like us, they don't appreciate their home being exposed to impending wet weather any more than you like your roof opened to the cold or wet elements.

- **They are busy with private matters.** Your bees may either be getting acquainted with a new queen while passing around her pheromones, getting her prepped for her mating flight, or there are other private matters going on to which you are not invited.

- **They don't like to be irritated.** If you are too noisy, too aggressive, or you have a distinct odor they don't like, your bees will let you know and may sting or bump you. They especially don't like garlic, bananas, perfume, body odor, and other distinct smells not of their hive. When they send out an alert pheromone, it has a banana-like odor. Odors clash with their hives' distinctive scents because each queen emits a different pheromone that is communicated throughout the hive. This is done by the bees using their antennae to touch the queen and then touching each hive member. They also use their wings to spread pheromone scents.

These pheromones are the hive's point of recognition and communication, and they help to create the hive's personality.

- **They only like short visits.** Even if your humming is sweet sounding and low, don't stay in the hive longer than 30 minutes. This invites other insects like wasps because of the honey smell. Bees keep their hives about 94°F and it often takes a lot to bring the hive back to the correct temperature. This is one of the reasons why opening the hive sets the bees back a whole day, not to mention stressing them.

We may never learn all the reasons why bees get agitated and that's okay. Just be sure to take notes if your bees do get aggravated so that you may possibly avoid the situation in the future.

Each hive will have very distinct personalities and sounds, and each hive will have different laying patterns according to its personality. If your hives are placed in the middle of geomagnetic lines, they may be arranged differently than the ones that were not placed in those grid lines. The electrical energy of the earth's geomagnetic lines may change from year to year. I made double-insulated topbar hives, and the brood nest stretched across the Langstroth frame the first year. The second year, the fall brood was laid in the front half with the nectar/honey toward the back. Keep notes on your hives and record everything from year to year. You may see a pattern change.

I have concluded that the bees communicating with us tells us what to expect in the environment and weather patterns. Each year, the bees teach me what to expect each season. I learned some of these subtleties while growing an organic garden in northern lower Michigan. I never used -cides, fertilizers, or any other soil enhancement other than my composted matter.

I discovered that plants work with the earth. If my tomatoes were more successful than the corn and potatoes, it was going to be a year of keeping my immune system up. Tomatoes have a lot of antioxidants and Vitamin C. If my potatoes and corn were more successful, we were going to have a long, cold winter and will need the carbohydrates to pad us to keep us warm.

By October, the bees will tell me what kind of winter we will have by how much stores they have and where they have put them. For example, one year, by the end of the last fall inspection I knew by where they had placed their stores when the beginning of winter would be hard and cold; would be more or less normal until the middle of winter when we would have a lot of warm days; then would be extremely cold. This information was conveyed when I viewed my notes the following spring. Starting from the east wall, the honey filled both sides of the frame next to the wall and on the second frame facing the wall (beginning of winter and into spring). Beebread was also heavy on the other side of the second frame and on both sides of the third frame (beginning of brood hatching). Remember there is honey at the top of each frame as well. Then frames four seemed to be stored with less. Frame five had more. Six had even less until. Seven had honey and some beebread. The eighth frame, next to the west wall, was empty. That was pretty much the way winter went.

Usually there are one to two frames of honey next to the west wall in the summer to help keep the hive cool and insulate from the hot western sun. In winter, the two frames next to the western wall may have some stores or none. I suspect it's so the hive can get all the heat that can be obtained.

Not all hives are going to communicate to you in this way. If you have about six or more colonies, you will see patterns of the way honey is stored. Again, it also depends on the genetics of the drones that mated with the queen. And it's going to take a while to learn how to look for this pattern. This is where keeping notes comes in handy.

Know About Bee Pheromones

Western or European honeybees (*Apis mellifera*) have one of the most complex pheromonal communication systems found in nature, possessing 15 known glands that produce an array of compounds. These chemical messengers are secreted by a queen, drones, worker bees, or a laying worker bee to elicit a response in other bees. The chemical messages are received by the bees' antennae and other body parts. They are produced as a volatile or non-volatile liquid and transmitted by direct contact as liquid or vapor; the vapor may be passed by flapping the wings.

Honeybee pheromones can be grouped into 1) releaser pheromones which temporarily affect the recipient's behavior, and 2) primer pheromones which have a long-term effect on the physiology of the recipient. Releaser pheromones trigger an almost immediate behavioral response from the receiving bee. Under certain conditions, a pheromone can act as both a releaser and a primer pheromone.

Pheromones in the hive are an important source of communication among the honeybees. They are used to identify the queen of a hive. If a worker of another hive tries to enter the hive with a different queen pheromone odor on her body, the bees will chase her out. The pheromones may either be single chemicals or a complex mixture of numerous chemicals in different percentages. Often, drones will stray in and are often accepted.

Entomologist, David Tarpy, NCSA, gave a lecture to our local bee club after attending a symposium on African bees. He shared that the reason an Africanized bee is able to kill a hive is because it has the intelligence to stand at the doorway or around other bees on the outside to get close enough for the hive's pheromones to get on her body. She will often dip in and out of the entrance for the same purpose. After a while, the Africanized bee will be able to get in unnoticed, find the queen, and kill her. This puts the hive into chaos and other

Africanized bees come in for the kill. I suspect yellow jackets can do the same since they can be similar in size of the honeybee. One of my first hives was killed by yellow jackets.

ALARM PHEROMONE

Two main alarm pheromones[xxix] have been identified in honeybee workers. One is released by the Koschevnikov gland, near the sting shaft, and consists of more than 40 chemical compounds. Alarm pheromones are released when a bee stings another animal. The released pheromone attracts other bees to the location and causes the other bees to behave defensively (i.e., sting or charge).

The other alarm pheromone is released by the mandibular glands and consists of 2-heptanone, which is also a highly volatile substance. This compound has a repellent effect, and it's proposed that this is used to deter potential enemies and robber bees. Bees use 2-heptanone as an anesthetic and to paralyze intruders before removing the paralyzed bees from the hive. Interestingly, the amounts of 2-heptanone increases with the age of bees and becomes higher in the case of foragers. This same pheromone will attract other bees to sting you almost immediately if you have already been stung. Smoke can mask the bees' alarm pheromone.

BROOD RECOGNITION PHEROMONE

Another pheromone is responsible for preventing worker bees from bearing offspring in a colony that still has developing young. Both larvae and pupae emit a *brood recognition* pheromone.[xxx] This inhibits ovarian development in worker bees and helps nurse bees distinguish worker larvae from drone larvae and pupae. The components of brood pheromone have been shown to vary with the age of the developing bee.

DRONE PHEROMONE

Drones produce a pheromone[xxxi] that attracts other flying drones to promote drone aggregations at sites suitable for mating with virgin queens. These sites are often referred to as the *drone bar*, but the correct term is "drone congregation area," aka DCA.

DUFOUR'S GLAND PHEROMONE

The DuFour's gland[xxxii] (named after the French naturalist Léon Jean Marie DuFour) opens into the dorsal vaginal wall. DuFour's gland and its secretion have been somewhat of a mystery. The gland secretes its alkaline products into the vaginal cavity, and it's assumed to be deposited on eggs as they are laid. Indeed, DuFour's secretions allow worker bees to distinguish between eggs laid by the queen, which are attractive, and those laid by workers. The complex of as many as 24 chemicals differs between workers in *queenright* colonies and workers of queenless colonies. In the latter, the workers' DuFour secretions are like those of a healthy queen. The secretions of workers in queenright colonies are long-chain alkanes with odd numbers of carbon atoms, but those of egg-laying queens and egg-laying workers of queenless colonies also include long chain esters.

EGG MARKING PHEROMONE

This pheromone, like that described above with DuFour's, helps nurse bees distinguish between eggs laid by the queen bee and eggs laid by a laying worker.

FOOTPRINT PHEROMONE

This pheromone is left by bees when they walk and is useful in enhancing Nasonov pheromones in searching for nectar.

In the queen, it is an oily secretion of the queen's tarsal glands that is deposited on the comb as she walks across it. This inhibits queen cell construction (thereby inhibiting swarming), and its production diminishes as the queen ages.

Forager Pheromone

Ethyl oleate is released by older forager bees to slow the maturing of nurse bees. This primer pheromone acts as a distributed regulator to keep the ratio of nurse bees to forager bees in the balance that is most beneficial to the hive.

Nasonov Pheromone

Nasonov pheromone[xxxiii] is emitted by the worker bees and used for orientation and recruitment. Nasonov pheromone includes many different terpenoids including geraniol, nerolic acid, citral, and geranic acid.

Other Pheromones

Other pheromones produced by most honeybees include rectal gland pheromone, tarsal pheromone, wax gland and comb pheromone, and tergite gland pheromone.

Queen Mandibular Pheromone

Queen mandibular pheromone (QMP)[xxxiv], emitted by the queen, is one of the most important sets of pheromones in the beehive. It affects social behavior, maintenance of the hive, swarming, mating behavior, and inhibition of ovary development in worker bees. The effects can be short and/or long term. Some of the chemicals found in QMP are carboxylic acids and aromatic compounds. Work on synthetic pheromones was patented in 1991.

Queen Retinue Pheromone

The following compounds have also been identified, of which only Coniferyl alcohol is found in the mandibular glands. There are nine compounds that make up Queen Retinue Pheromone (QRP)[xxxv] that are important for the retinue attraction of worker bees around their queen.

The queen also has an abundance of various methyl and ethyl fatty acid esters, very similar to the brood recognition pheromone described above. They are likely to have pheromonal functions like those found for the brood recognition pheromone.

Pheromones in the hive are used to communicate among the castes within the hive from the queen, to the drones, to the workers, and to calming bees. Essential oils in the hives not only destroy the bacterial balance in the hive, they interfere with the pheromones' communication and sets back the hive. All of it is traumatizing to the bee, which adds to the bees' stress level.

8: Honeybee Diseases and Pests

From pests to diseases, honeybees will always be dealing with something in their hives. This is Mother Nature's way of giving bees something against which they must build a defense system. Their immune system is 67 percent effective at best. The honeybee gut microbiota has bacteria to keep it healthy, but stress is the number one factor that will affect the microbiota to the point of illness. Therefore, to reiterate, the first premise in BEe Perspective beekeeping is keeping bees out of stress as much as possible. We have discussed the ways of entering into the hive and the when and how.

If your hive has survived more than a year, you have a good chance of keeping it longer by using the BEe Perspective methods. If, on the other hand, you have been treating your bees, you may not be able to stop as you have them trained for you to do their work.

The following are several diseases that you may encounter. They are listed in alphabetical order for easier reference.

Acarine Disease

Acarine Disease is caused by a tracheal mite called Acarapis Woodie. The mite lives in the respiratory system of adult bees and produces symptoms similar to Nosema. This disease is on its way out as it seems to have run its course.

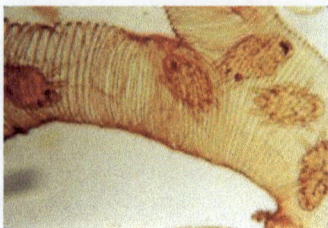

American Foulbrood (AFB)

American Foulbrood (AFB) is a spore-forming bacterium or *Paenibacillus larvae* (*P. Larvae*)[xxxvi] (formerly called *Bacillus larvae*) which are the most widespread and destructive of bee brood diseases. *P. Larvae* up to three days old become infected by ingesting spores present in their food. Young larvae less than 24 hours old are most susceptible to infection. Spores germinate in the gut of the larvae where the vegetative bacteria begin, taking nourishment from the larvae. Spores will not germinate in larvae over three days old. This disease only affects the bee larvae, but it is highly infectious and deadly to bee brood. Infected larvae darken and die after their cell is sealed. The vegetative form of the bacterium will die, but not before it produces about 100 million spores. American foulbrood spores are extremely resistant to desiccation and can remain viable for more than 40 years in honey and beekeeping equipment.

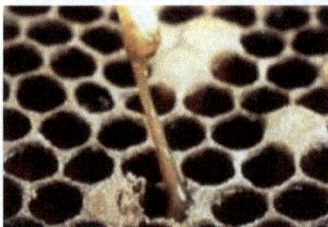

AFB produces a strong rotting odor in a cell with a sunken cap. When a toothpick is inserted into the cell cap and pulled out, there will be a mucilaginous string attached to it. Of the three foul smelling honeybee diseases, AFB has the worst odor.

Most states demand that you destroy your hive and your bees by burning everything. However, Les Crowder, a New Mexico Honeybee Inspector thinks otherwise. In his book, *Top Bar Beekeeping,* he expresses his opinion on this. His story begins with meeting an old-time beekeeper who was skeptical of Les. The passage in the book reads:

> "He asked me whether I was looking for foulbrood. When I said yes, he asked me what I would do if I found it. I told him that I felt that the beekeepers were using too many antibiotics in their hives and that I recommended re-queening with disease-resistant queens and getting rid of all of the old black combs, which usually got rid of the problem. His mood brightened when he heard that, and he told me that he was a retired doctor and that he'd done some research on the bacteria that reportedly caused foulbrood. He said, "Son, I looked up those bacteria and those bacteria are the pathogenic bacterial. They are putrefactive bacteria. I don't believe they cause the disease; they just decay the dead larvae.

> "I asked him what he thought caused the disease and he responded with, "The old black combs in the hive, particularly in the brood nest, are like us trying to stay healthy in a house full of sewage. Those old combs get thick and heavy – full of molds and bacteria. What you are calling disease-resistant bees are normal, old-fashioned, decent bees. What we have around here these days are bees with a genetic deficiency that makes their brood die. If you ever see your own hive sick with foulbrood, you should sterilize your hands and hive tool before you open the next hive so you don't spread the disease. I want you to try to spread the disease! Take combs full of sick larvae out of the sick hive, brush most of the bees off, and put the whole stinking comb in a healthy hive. Watch what happens to the healthy hive.

Keep trying if you want. I bet you won't be able to spread the disease, providing you don't fill up the hive with old black combs.

"A week later, I did find American Foulbrood in one of my hives. I decided to try Dr. Lyle's experiment. I shook most of the bees off and gave the comb full of dead, decaying larvae to a small, queen-mating nucleus hive. I chose this small hive because I didn't want to infect a big, honey-producing hive with the disease. I also thought that the small hive would be more rapidly impacted by the sick comb. It had a total of only four combs, and now one of them was filled with foulbrood infected larvae.

"One week later, I looked inside and there were no dead larvae or any other indications of foulbrood so the healthy combs and the foulbrood comb had very few sick larvae left. I thought that perhaps there might be an incubation period and that I hadn't waited long enough. When I checked again in another week the hive seemed disease-free, I gave it another infected comb and watched it all summer. It never got sick. I came to the conclusion that whether the larvae die of the bacteria or a genetic deficiency didn't matter. There are disease-resistant bees and when they received a sick comb in their midst, they simply clean it out. By culling old black comb from my hives and re-queening any hives that show signs of disease, I now rarely see any signs of foulbrood and have not used antibiotics for more than thirty years."

This is why it is a good idea to put colored thumb tacks on the top of your new frames that you put into your hive. The color code system goes in cycles every five years and will tell you when you should remove the old frame.

Chalkbrood Disease

Chalkbrood Disease is caused by a fungus called *Ascosphaera apis*. Initially, it is chalky-white but then looks like pieces of chalk in the comb. Some become dark blue-gray or almost black. Spores invade the larval tissues and kill the larvae after they have been capped. Chalkbrood Disease is usually more common on the edges of the brood nest where it is more susceptible to being chilled. Thus, it often attacks drone brood because they are located on the edge of the brood nest. Causes include stress, lack of ventilation, chilled brood, too much shade, and mold. Ventilation is the cure. This is why it is necessary to have the hive in at least six to eight hours of sun.

Chilled Brood

Photo by author

Chilled Brood is not caused by a virus or bacteria but rather by improper beekeeping practices. The name itself presents the cause which is hypothermia. In the picture to the left is how I found my hive the day after the lid blew off during a snow storm. You will find bees dead with their heads stuck in cells and other bees clinging to the comb, all dead. This can also happen when the winter cluster is too small to keep the cluster warm. The larvae on the comb in the picture will dry out and turn black. The most obvious symptom is death of all brood no matter its developmental stage with the brood on the comb edges most affected. It is the only brood condition that kills all brood within the hive and leaves the larvae black and shiny. [xxxvii]

European Foulbrood (EFB)

European Foulbrood (EFB) is a bacterium that infects the mid-gut of the bee larvae and is less serious than AFB. *Melissococcus plutonius (M. plutonius)* (sometimes called *Melissococcus pluton* and formerly called *Streptoccocus pluton)* is not spore-forming, and its cells can survive several months on wax foundation. Symptoms include dead and dying larvae which can appear curled upwards, brown, or yellow. It can also be melted or deflated with tracheal tubes more apparent or dried out and rubbery. This disease is the second disease that smells like something rotting.

EFB is often considered a *stress* disease — dangerous only if the colony is already under stress for other reasons and it is not arrested before it spreads too far. An otherwise healthy colony can usually survive EFB, but honey from treated colonies could have chemical residues from the treatment. Prophylactic treatments (chemicals) are not recommended as they lead to resistant bacteria. (NOTE: My Lacto formula is 100 percent effective and is in the Healing Formulas section in this book, along with the Honey Formula.)[xxxviii]

> *"It is supposed that lactobacilli, other lactic acid bacteria and bifidobacteria have a beneficial effect on honeybee health. For this reason, attempts to describe the occurrence of these bacteria in the digestive tract of these important pollinators have increased in recent years (Olofsson & Va´squez, 2008). Novel species of*

lactobacilli have been detected from the digestive tract of Apis mellifera and Apis dorsata (Olofsson & Va´squez, 2008; Tajabadi et al., 2011). The ability to inhibit in vitro the causal agent of American foulbrood (Paenibacillus larvae subsp. larvae) was found in these novel lactobacilli (Forsgren et al., 2010)."

Idiopathic Brood Disease Syndrome (IBDS)

Studies have shown that Glyphosate in Roundup® inhibits cytochrome P450 monooxygenases that detoxify insecticides in honeybees.[xxxix] These enzymes also detoxify phytochemicals, including the flavanol quercetin, in the bees' nectar-and pollen-based diet. Dr. Monika Krueger, Dr. of Veterinarian medicine at the Leipzig University, Germany, did a study on how the lactic acid is a critical factor in preventing intestinal colonization by *C. botulinum.*[xl] Among other studies she had done indicates that Glyphosate causes cows to prematurely abort their fetuses.

I live in a GMO farming community and had two hives on a farm that started growing GMO corn after I placed two bee hives on the edge of the corn field. In the first spring after the farmer used Roundup®, I found IBDS and EFB on one frame in each of those two hives. I know that *Lactobacilli* are as critical in the honeybee diet as it is in the human diet. What I don't know is if the lack of the LAB is the reason my bees got sick on that GMO farm. My hypothesis on IBDS in honeybees is that the cause comes from the glyphosate chemical in Roundup®. Since the honeybee larva cannot abort itself because it has nowhere to go, its only recourse is to rot in the cell.

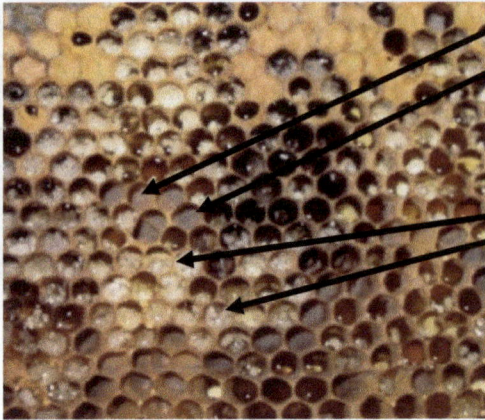

IBDS – Gray, lighter than charcoal, puddled mass with tip of larva head sticking up.

EFB – *M. plutonius*

Beige color; larva misshaped looking like lumps.

Photo by author.

It is possible to have two diseases existing in the hive. You can see the stress of IBDS caused EFB in my picture above . I didn't use the lacto formula because I thought anything rotting with IBDS will contain other bad bacteria. I didn't want my bees getting sick by cleaning the sprayed formula off the frames. I intuitively replaced the two frames that contained IBDS and EFB with new empty frames. There were no further issues. I threw out the comb and reused the frames. I did feed them the Honey formula to prevent further damage to the bees. You can read more in the Formula Section of this book.

Nosema Disease

Nosema Disease is caused by two species of microsporidian pathogens called *Nosema apis (N. apis)* and *Nosema cerana (N. cerana)* and are one-celled organisms that cause protozoan disease, now reclassified as a fungus.

Nosema is a fungus spore that invades the intestinal tracts of adult bees and causes diarrhea, also known as nosemosis. Nosema disorients the bees and in severe cases, many bees with unhooked wings are unable to fly and can be seen crawling in front of the hive. This is a general symptom of most adult bee diseases.

Nosema infection is also associated with black queen cell virus. Nosema is normally only a problem when the bees cannot leave the hive to eliminate waste, especially during an extended cold winter spell or when hives are enclosed in a wintering barn. When bees are unable to have their cleansing flights, they can develop dysentery.

Nosema is also caused by feeding bees plain sugar water. There are no nutrients in sugar water, including the good bacteria needed for a healthy gut and immune system. You may see a lot of brown spots on the outside of the beehive in winter and early spring. When there is a lack of *lactobacilli*, their gut is compromised. Just one feed of the Lacto formula or honey formula should take care of the problem. If they are out harvesting early spring, the early fresh nectar containing *lactobacilli* will also take care of the problem.

There are many types of BT products used by organic gardeners, and each type targets different insect groups such as beetles, mosquitoes, black flies, caterpillars, and moths. *Bacillus thuringiensis,* also known as BT, is a bacterium that makes proteins that are toxic to immature insects (larvae). BT bacterium itself will not harm humans or bees because of the acids in our stomachs. When Bt is ingested by a susceptible insect, the protein toxin is activated by alkaline conditions and enzyme activity in the insect's gut. If the activated toxin attaches to specific receptor sites, it paralyzes and destroys the cells of the gut wall, allowing the gut contents to enter the insect's body cavity.[xli] The proteins taken from the toxic gene in the BT bacteria are in every cell of GMO crop. A study done on BT toxins[xlii] in 2016 by Agricultural Sciences, University of Napoli, Italy, indicates that a weakened immune system of an insect is far more susceptible to the toxic gene in BT bacterium. Exposure to toxic gene in corn pollen (GMO corn) containing this toxin will weaken the bees' defense against Nosema. *Lactobacilli* strengthens the immune system.

Because I live in a GMO farming community, this disease is another reason I may feed my bees once with my honey formula in the in the spring when farmers and gardeners use herbicides. I will also feed them the formula in the fall when I think they are harvesting pollen from the GMO crops. The *lactobacilli* bacteria in the honey formula will prevent Nosema. When fed in the fall, the bees will add the honey formula to their pollen. The following spring, I know the bees will feed on beebread with the good bacteria in the honey formula.

The Canadian company, Medivet Pharmaceuticals Ltd., was the only company that sold Fumagillin-B, an antimicrobial used to treat Nosema.[xliii] This company closed its doors in 2018.

Black Queen Cell Virus (BQCV)

Black Queen Cell Virus (BQCV) causes the queen larva to turn black and die. It is thought to be associated with Nosema.

Photo: Rob Snyder, BeeInformed.org

Small Hive Beetle

The small beehive beetle (*Aethina tumida*) is a small, dark-colored beetle. They burrow through brood comb, but they have also been found on clean wax as well.

In the picture to the left, you'll see a comb slimed by hive beetle larvae. Hives infested at this level will drive out bee colonies.

Photo: Wikipedia

The dark circles in the picture to the right are what small hive beetles (SHB) look like.

Photo: Keeping Backyard Bees

When you see many SHB, it is usually a sign of a weak hive. It is a good idea to take what bees that are left and put them into a nuc. The same applies to Wax Moths (which you'll read about further). A natural method for SHB is to place in the hive a small container filled with unpasteurized apple cider vinegar (ACV), preferably organic. It's been recorded to work well. The small amount of ACV you put in your honey formula will not affect the SHB.

As discussed in another section of the book, you may use geomagnetic lines to protect your bees from pests such as mites and beetles. This can be done by placing your hive in the middle of a grid line of geomagnetic lines. The vibrating hertz of beetles and Varroa are much lower than the honeybee. Mites and beetles don't like to live in an environment with a high energy of 190-250 hertz.

Stonebrood Disease

Stonebrood Disease is caused by two fungi, called *Aspergillus flavus* and *Aspergillus fumigatus*, which looks very similar to Chalkbrood Disease. Affected capped cells often contain a small puncture usually about the size of a pinhead. When first affected, larvae are dull and grey in color. They then turn slightly yellow with a dark head and become brown after a few days, eventually turning almost black. The *Chinese clipper* or *canoe* shape of dead larvae is characteristic of this disease. During the period of decay, the outer skin of the dead larvae toughens. Note of curiosity: *Aspergillus fumigatus* is the same fungus that creates Fumagillin[xliv] [xlv], a product used to make Fumagillin-B.

This disease looks very similar to Chalkbrood, which is soft and crushable. Stonebrood is the opposite; it is as hard as stone. Stonebrood is also usually caused by the reasons your bees develop Chalkbrood.

Varroa Destructor (Varroa Mite)

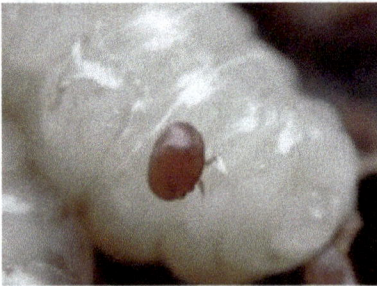

Varroa destructor is different from *Varroa jacobsoni* and is a parasitic mite that feeds on the bodily fluids of adult larvae and bees. Varroa can be seen with the naked eye as a small red or brown spot on the bee's thorax. These mites are carriers for a virus that is particularly damaging to bees. Bees infected with this virus during their development will often have visibly deformed wings that can be seen after the bee hatches.

Varroa have led to the virtual elimination of feral bee colonies in many areas and are a major problem for kept bees in apiaries. Some feral populations are now recovering — it appears they have been naturally selected for Varroa resistance. It's my theory that the feral bees were not interfered with or treated and thus evolved into healthier colonies.

V. jacobsoni was noted for the first time in 1904, in the nest of *Apis cerana.* The first Varroa mites were probably found in Korea (1950) and next in Japan (1958). In the following years, they have spread all over the world. At the time, they were regarded as *V. jacobsoni.* They were discovered in the United States in 1987, in New Zealand in 2000, and in Devon, United Kingdom in 1992. Recently, Anderson and Trueman have proved that V. *jacobsoni* is more than one species. They gave the new name *Varroa destructor n. sp.* to the group of six haplotypes. Mites, which became pests of *Apis mellifera* worldwide, belong to *V. destructor.*[xlvi]

These mites are generally not a problem for a strong, growing hive. When the hive population is reduced in preparation for winter or due to poor late summer forage, the Varroa can overtake bees and destroy the hive. Under such conditions, the colony will often simply abscond (leave as in a swarm with no population behind).

Varroa, in combination with deformed wing virus and bacteria, have theoretically been implicated in colony collapse disorder. I have my own theories on CCD.

Viruses are pieces of genetic material that parasitize a host cell, making the cell produce more viruses. Many viruses can be directly transmitted by Varroa mites. No vaccines or medications are available for any of the honeybee viruses. Therefore, good sanitation practices are the key to prevention. It is said that comb replacement and re-queening are the best practical responses to a virus infection. I will argue the re-queening factor.

Treating a hive with antibiotics too often for "just-in-case" or a virus, as beekeepers do, will weaken the honeybees' immune systems, thereby weakening the colony. If the hive had diverse genetics with hygienic behaviors, kept stress-free, and placed between geomagnetic gridlines, it would be unlikely the colony would have Varroa issues. Treating any living element with unnatural substances too often will weaken it to the point of it not being able to take care of itself.

The following viruses are related to the *Varroa destructor* and can be either chronic or acute:[xlvii]

CHRONIC BEE PARALYSIS VIRUS (CBPV)

Chronic bee paralysis virus (CBPV) was one of the first honeybee viruses to be isolated. Due to the infection, it is the only common honeybee virus to have both visual behavior and physiological modifications. Symptoms of the disease are observed in adult bees displaying one or two sets of symptoms called Syndromes.

Syndrome 1 includes abnormal trembling of the wings and body. The bees cannot fly and often crawl on the ground and up plant stems. In some cases, crawling bees can be found in large numbers (1000+). The bees huddle together on top of the cluster or on the top bars of the hive. They may have bloated abdomens due to distension of the honey sac. The wings are partially spread or dislocated.

Photo: The Food and Environment Research Agency (FERA)

With Syndrome 2, infected bees can fly but are almost hairless. They appear dark or black, shiny, and smaller than average honeybees. Their abdomens are relatively broad. Older bees in the colony often nibble on them, and this may be

110

the cause of hairlessness. They are hindered at the entrance to the hive by the guard bees. A few days after infection, trembling begins. They then become flightless and soon die.

ACUTE BEE PARALYSIS VIRUS (ABPV)

Acute Bee Paralysis Virus (ABPV) is a common infective agent of bees. It belongs to the family Dicistroviridae as does the Israel Acute Paralysis Virus (IAPV), Kashmir Bee Virus (KBV), and the Black Queen Cell Virus (BQCV). It is frequently detected in healthy colonies, and it plays a role in cases of sudden collapse of honeybee colonies infested with *Varroa destructor*.

IAPV seems to be the most destructive as described in a 2014 study published in the Public Library of Services (PLoS): [xlviii]

> *"Microarray profiles of host responses to IAPV infection revealed that mitochondrial function is the most significantly affected biological process, suggesting that viral infection causes significant disturbance in energy-related host processes. The expression of genes involved in immune pathways in adult bees indicates that IAPV infection triggers active immune responses."*

CLOUDY WING VIRUS (CWV)

Cloudy Wing Virus (CWV) is a little-studied, small, icosahedral virus commonly found in honeybees, especially in collapsing colonies infested by *Varroa destructor*, providing circumstantial evidence that the Varroa may act as a vector. Wings appear cloudy or opaque.

DEFORMED WING VIRUS (DWV)

Deformed Wing Virus (DWV) is the cause of wing deformities and other body malformations typically seen in honeybee colonies that are heavily infested with the parasitic mite *Varroa*

destructor. DWV is part of a complex and closely related virus strain/specie that also includes Kakugo virus, *Varroa destructor* virus 1, and Egypt Bee Virus. This deformity can clearly be seen on the honeybee's wings in the image. The deformities are produced almost exclusively due to DWV transmission by *Varroa destructor* when it parasitizes pupae. Bees infected as adults remain symptom-free, although they do display behavioral changes and have reduced life expectancy. Deformed bees are rapidly expelled from the colony, leading to a gradual loss of adult bees for colony maintenance. If this loss is excessive and can no longer be compensated by the emergence of healthy bees, the colony rapidly dwindles and dies.

SACBROOD DISEASE

Photo: Robert Snyder, BeeInformed.org

Sacbrood disease is viral, caused by Perina Nuda Picorna-like Virus (PNPV), an insect-infecting RNA virus. Affected larvae change from pearly white to gray and finally black.

Utah County Beekeepers Association

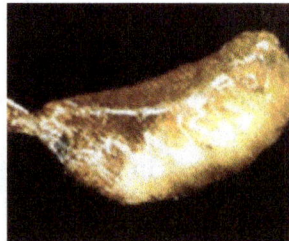

Death occurs when the larvae are upright just before pupation. Consequently, affected larvae are usually found in capped cells. Head development of diseased larvae is typically retarded. The head region is usually darker than the rest of the body and may lean toward the center of the cell. When affected larvae are carefully removed from their cells, they appear to be a sac filled with water. Typically, the scales are brittle but easy to remove. Sacbrood-diseased larvae have no characteristic odor. It is often believed to be spread by feeding contaminated pollen, nectar, or water to young larvae.

Wax Moths

There are two species of wax moth:

Lesser Wax Moth - Galleria mellonella.

en.wikipedia.org/wiki/Lesser wax moth

Greater Wax Moth - Achroia grisella

n.wikipedia.org/wiki/Galleria_mellonella

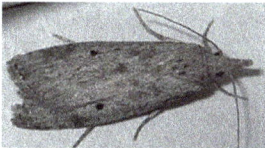

https://de.wikipedia.org/wiki/Wachsmotten

Wax moths eat beeswax, pollen, remains of larval honeybees, honeybee cocoon silk, and enclosed honeybee feces found on walls of brood cells. They will not attack the bees directly. But they attack weak hives and feed on wax used by bees to build their honeycomb. The used brood comb or brood cell cleanings are needed for wax moths to develop into full adults. The brood cells contain protein essential for the larval development, in the form of brood cocoons. The destruction of the comb will spill or contaminate stored honey and may kill bee larvae. Wax moth larvae looks similar to SHB larvae.

If the honeybee's immune system is compromised, it will allow other negative factors to interfere and weaken it, similar to humans. Taking into consideration that most destructive diseases have their elements in the gut section of the bee, does it not make sense to make sure their immune system is as high as it should be? This weakened immune system causes a weak colony that cannot take care of itself, allowing pests and diseases to invade the hive.

You can treat for wax moths with traps and commercial products, but you wouldn't be taking care of the cause. Chances are, by the time you found the problem, it has gone beyond treatment. Let the hive die honorably and freeze the frame with wax, with the box if possible, in a freezer for at least 24 to 36 hours. The freezing will kill any eggs left in the hive equipment, especially those eggs hidden in tiny crevices and holes.

The wax moth, also known as the Greater Wax Moth, has a gut enzyme that is presently being studied as a solution for breaking down polyethylene, the plastic that has polluted our environments. The plastic foundation coated with wax was created and used in 1964. As I have said before, Mother Nature has a way of getting Her revenge. It would seem that with the wax moth eating on the honeycomb all these past years may have evolved to eating the plastic foundation in frames as well.

Scientists are considering using the Greater Wax Moth for our plastic pollution. Considering a single wax moth female can lay 300 eggs that hatch to the larval state between five to eight days, can you imagine what they would have to do once the plastic is gone and we are left with the worms? I suspect our scientists will invent a reason for another chemical to rid a problem they created.

NOTE: In Apitherapy, we teach that you can actually eat bee, SHB, and wax moth larvae. It's called Apilarnil.

A final Note:

Dr. Jamie Ellis, PhD, the Gahan Associate Professor of Entomology in the Department of Entomology and Nematology at the University of Florida, spoke at the Center for Honeybee Research's New Frontier Seminar in November

2010 on *Varroa destructor*. I was interested in some of his research and asked him more questions about the disease via email correspondence. You may find his response to me interesting and helpful in the following:

> *"... At the end of the day, it's ok with me if you tell your audiences that research from a bee scientist at the University of Florida showed that treating bees with Fumagillin did not control Nosema in a Florida apiary and that 3 commercially-available honeybee diets did not benefit colony strength parameters for test bee colonies in FL. Hope this helps."*

9: Healing Formulas

I live in a farming community where glyphosate in Roundup®, Rodeo®, and other brands, are used throughout the beekeeping season by farmers, railroad companies, and the utility company. These herbicides' residual spray stays in the wind and travels for miles and miles until the rain washes the chemicals into the ground. While traveling in the air, this residual spray will stick to plants that bees encounter when harvesting nectar and pollen. The bees then take this chemical back to the hive and spread it around by walking on the honeycomb. The glyphosate changes or kills the good bacteria. The bees know something is wrong and get stressed. This stress develops into EFB and I must use my Lacto formula to take care of it.

Back in 2012, I began collaborating with Dr. Don Huber, Emeritus Professor at Purdue University and plant pathologist. My bees gave me the idea of using probiotics, which I knew were important for the immune system. Don helped me to understand about how and why *Lactobacillus* is vital to the immune system in all living elements on the earth, in the earth, and for humans in a way I didn't understand before.

Glyphosate's destruction to human and animal health is enormous. It kills *Lactobacilli* in the soil that protects plants from taking up the *Clostridium botulinum* group of bacteria which includes *salmonella*, *listeria*, and *E. coli*. Without the protection of *Lactobacilli*, the *botulinum* bacteria come up through the plants; and ingesting the bacterium causes digestive disorders that can cause various illnesses. Since the *Lactobacilli* cannot reach the plant's nectar or pollen, the beneficial bacteria will not be available to honeybees or any other pollinators. While no single bacterium is healing by itself, most support each other and the immune systems in everything living.

In the 1990s, five chemicals were added to nicotinoids and the name was changed to neonicotinoids, or Neonics.[xlix] This group of insecticides is used to coat GMO seeds and some non-GMO seeds like canola and work synergistically with glyphosate in killing our pollinators. Bees love corn pollen. Come winter, the hatching bees are fed the beebread made from the pollen of the GMO corn harvested the previous fall. You can have an active hive one week only to have a dead or empty hive in less than two weeks later.

Two of the five chemicals in Neonics are deadly to the bees. Clothianidin[l] affects the worker honeybees' learning ability. She will go out to harvest nectar and pollen but will forget how to make it back to her hive. Imidacloprid affects the queen bee's endocrine system, thereby affecting her egg-laying abilities. I saw this in my apiary in 2011 before hearing Dr. Don Huber and Dr. Mercola on YouTube speaking about the effects of Roundup®. I contacted Don and, thus, started my journey into researching -*cides* and a valuable friendship.

As an Apitherapist, I had a pretty good idea of what was in honey. More research indicated how honey's density and bacterial content helped to preserve it. I knew there was a way to use beehive products for whatever diseases the honeybees have. After all, they have been fighting diseases and pests for thousands of years. I had an epiphany moment and contacted Don again. He enlightened me on the effects of pH for good bacteria growth and how it would create the growth.

The Importance of pH Levels

According to Parasitology Research:

> *"All members of the Animalia kingdom, including humans, have helpful symbiotic microbiotas which are extremely important for the proper functioning of the gastrointestinal tract. These symbiotic microorganisms are responsible for the fermentation of carbohydrates as well as the production of some vitamins and amino acids that their hosts need. Furthermore, gut microbiota, through the "barrier effect," prevent pathogenic microorganisms from colonizing the gastrointestinal tract. In particular, Lactic acid bacteria (LAB) prove to be important inhabitants of animal and human intestinal tracts as they have a multifaceted, antimicrobial potential, mainly because of their ability to synthesize lactic acid, short-chain, volatile fatty-acid, and bacteriocin-like molecules (Jack et al. 1995; Wilson et al. 2005; Audisio et al. 2011). Lactic acid bacteria are usually considered probiotics, i.e., viable microorganisms that provide health benefits to their hosts."*[li]

Lactobacillus and *Bifidobacterium* are two important bacteria strains that are naturally found in every living thing on earth including air, soil, insects, animals, humans, as well as the honeybees.[lii] These bacteria are extremely important for health. In humans, *Lactobacillus* constitute a significant component of microbiota in several locations of the body including the digestive system, urinary system, and genital system. *Bifidobacteria* are ubiquitous inhabitants of the gastrointestinal tract, vagina, and mouth. They are also the major genera of bacteria that make up the colon. *Bifidobacteria* protect the *Lactobacilli* in the human digestive tract.

Even though the honeybees don't have a digestive system with small and large intestines, they do have the need for both

Lactobacilli and *Bifidobacteria* bacteria in their guts. Bees collect *Lactobacilli* when they harvest nectar and keep the harvest in their honey crop (stomach). (*Lactobacillus* is a lactic acid (LAB) that ferments honey when water is added.) Every time the bee gurgitates the nectar, they add additional bacteria to the honey. This process of transferring honey from one bee to another is called the "honey kiss" The kiss helps to take out the excess water and bring the honey down to about 18 percent water content. The LAB in the honey slowly breaks down the pollen's outer layer and ferments the pollen to make beebread. There is not enough water in the honey to ferment it once the honey is sealed in the cell. The honey's low water, LAB, and pH are part of the reasons why honey does not go bad.

Honey is the bee's prebiotic while the beebread is their probiotic and protein. Yet, both hive products contain these bacteria along with yeasts, vitamins, minerals, enzymes, and more beneficial nutrients. A probiotic is a substance that stimulates the growth of microorganisms, especially those with beneficial properties. It stimulates a healthy immune response in the honeybee as well as in humans and other living organisms. 7.0 pH is mid-point on the pH scale. Anything lower than 7.0 pH is acidic and anything higher is alkaline. [liii] Good bacteria grow in an acidic pH below 5.0 and will grow between 94° and 97° F – the same temperature of the human body and honeybee hive.

When using honey in sugar feed with the Apple Cider Vinegar (ACV) to bring the pH down to equal honey's 4.3-4.5 pH, you also add the other nutrients and chemicals that are in the ACV in medicinal and perhaps homeopathic doses to aid the honeybees in their fight against other diseases. Formic Acid and Oxalic Acid obtained from nectar are in the honey and will naturally fight Varroa by the larvae ingesting the honey from within the cell.

A healthy honeybee will have upwards of 186 different bacterial strains in its stomach[liv] and all grow in different pH environments. *Lactobacillus plantarum (L. Plantarum)* is one of two strains of bacteria that has been shown to kill AFB.[lv] The other is *Lactobacillus kunkeei (L. kunkeei)* which grows at 4.5 to 6.8 pH and prefers fructose that is contained in wine, flowers, and honey. Both strains are carried in the bee's stomach. *L. plantarum* poses a curious natural phenomenon as it acidifies a growth medium to a low 2.0 to 4.0 pH within several hours.[lvi] So even though you start out with 5.0 pH with the ACV, the *plantarum* bacteria will take the pH down to include the *L. kunkeei* bacteria to help with AFB. Using fructose honey harvested in spring and early summer is best.

During the dearth, a time when there are no or very few blooms, aphids will prick leaves and drink the sap. Their sweet feces are picked up by the honeybees and taken back to the hive and made into honey. This is called Honeydew Honey and is full of extra minerals, but not always that great for growing the right bacteria. It also contains particles not easily digestible for young bees.

Other bacterial strains fermented by LAB also help with the honeybee's immune system.[lvii]

> *"The use of Lactobacillus species as probiotics has been found to enhance the immunity of honeybees, helping them to survive against the effect of pathogens and bring advantageous properties for honeybee health."*

When my bees first contracted EFB, I used a commercial probiotic which proved extremely effective. I used capsules containing eight strains at 30 billion CFUs added to water to create what I refer to as my lacto water. However, I changed my formula after learning that *Lactobacillus casei (L. casei)* is required by everything living. Once I added the 10-strain probiotic to the sugar water feed, my bees seemed to be happier than using just the eight-strain formula. These bacteria will also grow in just a few hours at 94° F. Below is one of the research studies I used to create my Lacto water formula for EFB: [lviii]

"Also, in beekeeping management, there are commercial diet supplements which contain probiotics and/or prebiotics. One such supplement recommended for the feeding of honeybees and other animals contains bacteria such as L. casei, L. plantarum, Rhodopseudomonas palustris, and yeast Saccharomyces cerevisiae. A further example, in addition to lactic acid bacteria (Lactobacillus acidophilus or L. casei) and Bifidobacterium lactis, also comprises prebiotics."

When you make sugar feed with your own water, assuming your water is at 7.0 pH, you need to take the pH level down. Mold will grow in 7.0 pH and is one of the reasons bees develop Nosema in the spring when sugar water alone is fed. ACV will bring the pH level down to 4.3 - 4.5 to equal honey's pH before it is capped.

There are beekeepers using distilled vinegar, otherwise known as white vinegar, because the wasps won't bother the sugar feed with distilled vinegar. This should be a red flag for beekeepers. Spirit or white distilled vinegar is made by the acetic fermentation of diluted distilled alcohol (ethanol). The alcohol in the hard cider is what transforms via fermentation in acetic acid, which is the beneficial organic compound that gives apple cider vinegar its sour taste.[lix] The difference between distilled vinegar and ACV is that the ACV has natural probiotics that are easier on the bee's intestinal tract.[lx] Honeybees are trusting creatures and don't know the difference.

Honey's low water content is one of the key factors to why it doesn't spoil. When you add water to honey, it starts to ferment immediately. Because of its fermentation properties, honey is used for honey wine called mead. Instead of using ground-up raisins, honey is used to make some herbal wines, like dandelion wine. Therefore, I like to add one-half pint of honey to about three-quarters of a gallon of sugar water so that some of the LABs and *Bifidobacterium* already in the honey will grow. The honey also adds other vital nutrients for the honeybee's immune system. I then add my tablespoon of homemade ACV to bring down the pH. I do this based on the hypothesis that the *L. plantarum* grows and lowers the pH for the *L. kunkeei*[lxi] to grow and continues to multiply the good bacteria the longer it sits. Sometimes, you will see bubbles grow on top of the solution. This is a sign of good fermentation. The water should be no cooler than your body temperature when adding the ACV.

Two Formulas

I feed my bees the Honey Formula in their sugar feed and lightly spritz the frames with the lacto water if there is evidence of EFB. Also, I feed my bees when my neighbors spray herbicides under their sheep fence. The following formulas have never failed me and the lacto water works within 10 minutes. I tested this with an EFB kit. Best of all, it is 100 percent effective.

IMPORTANT NOTE: Do not combine the store-bought probiotic with the honey formula. Just like humans, bees may develop diarrhea with too much probiotics.

METHOD 1: LACTO WATER

When buying store-bought probiotics, be sure it contains several strands of *Lactobacilli* and *Bifidobacterium*, especially *L. casei*.

Step 1: Get the Probiotic Solution Ready

- With one cup of room temperature (tepid) water, empty the contents of one commercial probiotic capsule (preferably 10 strains of *Lactobacillus* that includes *L. casei* and *Bifidobacterium*, 30 billion CFUs). The next page shows the list of probiotics I use.

Bifidobacterium lactis	
Bifidobacterium breve	
Bifidobacterium longum	
Total Bifido Probiotic Cultures	**18 billion**
Lactobacillus acidophilus	
Lactobacillus casei	
Lactobacillus plantarum	
Lactobacillus paracasei	
Lactobacillus salivarius	
Lactobacillus rhamnosus	
Lactobacillus bulgaricus	
Total Lacto Probiotic Cultures	**12 billion**
Total Bifido/Lacto Cultures	**30 billion**

- Stir for a few minutes until dissolved.

- Refrigerate when not using.

- Do not keep this solution beyond 4 to 5 days as it deteriorates. Go to Step 2.

Step 2: Get the Sugar Water Solution Ready

- Add 11 cups of white sugar to a glass gallon container. Don't use organic sugar as it contains solid particles that honeybees cannot digest.

- Add about a quart of hot water (not quite boiling) to dissolve the sugar.

- Stir until the sugar crystals are dissolved.

- Add enough cold water to fill the container to within 1-inch from the top to bring the temperature down to about 95°F, or when it feels comfortable when you touch the container with your hands. Go to Step 3.

Step 3: Combining the Probiotic and Sugar Water Solution

- When the sugar water solution is cooled to 95°F, add 2 tablespoons of the lacto formula. If the water is hotter than body temperature, you will destroy the probiotics.

- Stir well.

- Feed your bees immediately if the weather will not allow you to wait. It is better if you wait three hours for the sugar to grow more bacteria.

Lacto Water to Treat EFB

In a quart spray bottle, add one teaspoon of the lacto water to a pint of tepid water. Lightly spritz both sides of all frames, especially those filled with brood and larvae as well as the sides of boxes in the hive body. You don't need to spray the bottom board or inner cover (unless they are solid) or the top outer cover. The EFB is affected immediately.

But because EFB is a bacterial growth and you cannot be assured of getting all of it in one spray, repeat every four days for about two to four weeks until there is no longer any odor from the hive when you open it. It may take longer if there is a lot of rain or a damp, humid environment. This is another reason I don't smoke bees. The smell of smoke prevents me from smelling hive contents. You will notice the rotting smell decreases after the first use. If you catch EFB in the early stages, as on one frame, you can eradicate the EFB in just one or two sprays. The affected larvae will dry up in the cells and the bees will carry them out of the hive. The lacto water will not harm unaffected larvae or bees.

NOTE: You will also need to feed your bees the lacto sugar water or honey formula and perhaps some pollen, during this time if there is not enough in the hive. Bees are just like you when they are ill. They don't want to do much and are not too functional outside the hive. Once EFB starts to die off, the bees will become more active and start to forage again in a very short time.

METHOD 2: HONEY FORMULA

When growing your own *Lactobacilli*, I wouldn't suggest using nectar as it is not a complete product as honey. The process of drying honey is done by the bees batting their wings and exchanging nectar amongst themselves using their proboscis, during which time they put in vitamins, minerals, acids, yeasts, hydrogen peroxide, and other good magic. Once the honey is about 18 percent water, they cap it off during the night.

Step 1: Get the Sugar Water Solution Ready

- Add 11 cups of white sugar to a glass gallon container. Don't use organic sugar as it contains minute solid particles that honeybees cannot digest.

- Add about a quart of hot water (not quite boiling) to dissolve the sugar.

- Stir until the sugar crystals are dissolved.

    - Add about a pint of cool water to cool the sugar water solution down to a temperature that is comfortable when you touch the container. Go to Step 2.

Step 2: Adding Honey to the Sugar Water Solution

- Be sure the container is out of sunlight. Never put any honey in the sunlight as the nectar comes from the same plant source often used for medicinal purposes. Sunlight and heat will destroy the

126

healing properties of harvested plants, so goes with hive products, including honey. Add ½ to 1 pint of honey, preferably organic or from a treatment-free beekeeper, and 1 tablespoon of ACV. The ACV will bring down the pH, the LAB in the honey will work together and start fermenting.

- Add enough tepid water to fill the glass gallon container to within 1-inch from the top.

- Stir the mixture again. You may notice bubbles in the solution at the top rim after it has sat for two to three hours, sometimes sooner. This is good.

- Feed your bees immediately if the weather will not allow you to wait. It is better if you wait three hours for more bacteria to grow.

- During the warmest part of the day, feed your bees. Don't let the solution set for too long. In a couple of days, you will smell alcohol which is the product made from the fermentation. You can usually still feed the bees the fermented formula, though I don't recommend it.

10: The Second Year

The second year of beekeeping is filled with another set of parameters to learn. You will need to inspect your hives and watch for certain conditions to know when and if you should make a split.

Inspecting Your Hives

The queen starts laying eggs the day after winter solstice. Your hive will increase little by little according to the weather and the colony's needs, and your bees will begin harvesting pollen and nectar, mainly from trees, as early as January.

YOUR INSPECTION

In mid-January, check the weight of your hive. If you have a two-to-three box hive body and it is an eight-frame Langstroth, it should weigh a minimum of about 30 pounds. If it doesn't, then you may not have enough stores. This is dependent upon the size of your bees, the size of the cluster, how the winter went, etc. You can check the weight by using your one hand to lift the back of the hive up about an inch or two. I prefer a top-feeder that sits on the hive under the inner cover because it allows the bees access to food within the hive.

If you don't have feeders, you may also use a square two-inch tall spacer that can be placed on the hive box, also called a shim, made out of ¾ inch lumber. Place it on top of the top box and under the inner cover and feed them the honey formula in a plastic gallon bag laid on top of the frames with a slit cut into the side of the bag. I don't recommend entrance feeders as I've never found them successful. In fact, they are usually messy as they attract robbers, and the bees must go through the hive's entrance to feed.

Mid to Late February Inspection

In mid to late February and weather permitting, make weekly inspections to check how fast your colony is growing. Whether you have an eight-or 10-frame Langstroth, split your hive when there are about two frames left to fill – unless you don't care if your bees swarm. It is the honeybee's nature to swarm for more room and to multiply their species. Sadly, only about 20 percent of swarms survive which is why I recommend making splits.

Splitting Your Hives

When making a split, choose four frames with eggs, larvae, and capped and uncapped brood and place them in a nuc box after closing the entrance to prevent bees from leaving. Check where the queen is located so that you can leave her behind in the original hive box. As you transfer the frames into a nuc box, also be sure to keep the nurse bees on the frames. If you have it, add one frame of honey with bee bread/pollen. Nurse bees don't do any harvesting and need the food for themselves and for the bees that hatch. If you don't have the extra frame of food, put in an empty frame strung with fishing line or with comb to make up the five-frame nuc. Take a few frames from out of the hive body and shake in some extra bees into the nuc box. Put on the top lid and take the nuc at least two miles away to another site. I prefer five driven miles away, which is not necessarily bee miles. I use a ratchet strap to keep the hive together during transportation.

The bees usually graft about three to seven larvae, not eggs, that are about 24 to 36 hours old and raise them as queens. As the queens grow, the cells take on a peanut-shell shape and grow out and down on a frame.

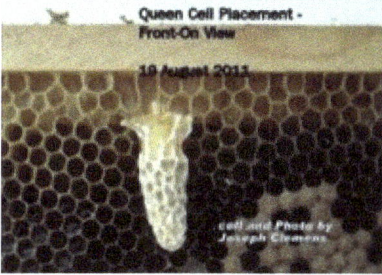

Photo: cookevillebeekeepers.com
Queen cell placed in the comb.

The picture to the left shows a queen cell that had been cut out and placed on a comb.

Photo: mistressbeek.com
Natural combs.

In the picture to the right is a natural queen cell and a queen cup located in the upper left of the queen cell.

Photo: beegood.co.uk

You will read that a queen cell in the center of a frame, as in the picture to the left, is called a *supersedure cell*, meaning they are going to re-queen because the bees want a different queen or after a split has been made.

131

If the queen cells are at the bottom of a frame, as shown in the picture to the right, or the cells are of different ages, it may mean the bees are going to swarm. Once they get it in their heads to swarm, it is often too late to make a split. Another good indication they are going to swarm is the increased amount of drone cells.

It boggles my mind when some beekeepers enter their hives and pinch or cut out several queen cells until about two are remaining. Even the worker bees don't kill a queen in a queen cell. If your hive is struggling or if there is not enough pollen, young bees may not be able to make enough quality royal jelly to feed the queen in the cells and may fill it with worker jelly. You may also see capped, stunted queen cells. No matter how many there are, just leave the queen cells alone.

The first queen that hatches out will go around and chew a hole into the sides of all of the other queen cells and sting the queen larvae inside the cells. The worker bees then remove the dead larvae and will have all the cells broken down in about 24 hours. On rare occasions, you may find a sister queen in the same hive. Don't kill her. She is there by permission of the colony.

Once you make a split, do not go into the nuc for at least 14 to 16 days. The frames will be tight. If you pull it out within that time frame, you are apt to tear the one queen cell you may have and there goes your chance of having another colony. If this happens, you will either have to put the frames back into the original hive or get another frame containing nurse bees and eggs from another hive and place it into the nuc and wait another 14 to16 days.

Some beekeepers will order queens if they don't find one in their hives. This takes time and you will risk the hive will develop a laying worker. You can tell a laying worker by how the eggs are placed into the cell. Often there is more than one egg in one cell, and the eggs will be on the side wall of the cell – not in the bottom on the rhomboid. A laying worker can only lay drones as she has never mated. Your best bet is to put in a frame or two of brood with uncapped larvae and eggs.

After waiting 14 to16 days to check your queen, you may or may not be able to recognize her. As a virgin queen, she is about the same size as a worker bee, but with a longer, more pointed abdomen. The time it takes for the queen to mate and lay eggs will depend on various factors:

- It takes about three days for a queen to finish her transformation, or harden, after hatching. Her color changes and her exoskeleton becomes less flexible, hardens.

- A queen may take another three or four days to prep for her mating flight.

- If the weather is a downpour, a queen will wait until she can fly to mate.

- After mating, it takes about three or four days for her spermatheca to swell and her abdomen to enlarge.

After making a split, I have waited as long as 29 days due to a long rainy month.

Mating Your Queen

One of the most important elements in good beekeeping is creating and keeping diverse genetics. If you keep all your bees in the same yard, you don't know if they are mating with their cousins or not. Some refer to these bees as Buckfast Bees,[lxii] a breed of honeybees crossed by many subspecies and their strains. This strain was developed by Brother Adam *(born Karl   Kehrle in 1898 in Germany)*, who was in charge of beekeeping from 1919 at Buckfast Abbey in Devon in the United Kingdom.

Part of the problem of declining honeybees today is that there are only a handful of people making commercial queens. Watering down the gene pool is when queens are mated with the same breed of drones every year and usually in the same area, or drone yards. Mating a queen from one climate zone and moving her to another climate zone is not healthy. It would be like taking someone who has lived a lifetime in warm, sunny Florida and moving that person to the frigid parts of Alaska.

When you're ready to mate your queen, take your nuc up the road about five miles. This allows her to mate with drones from another area, thereby making for a diverse colony. You hope she is a hussy and mates with at least 12 drones; hopefully up to 20 drones. The drone carries the genetic markers for a honeybee. The more different drones you have, the more diverse the genes. In mountainous ranges where I live, three miles may be enough, assuming you know there are enough drones in the area. Remember, you are driving those miles. The bees shorten the distance when flying.

When you know the new queen is laying, close up the nuc's entrance after dusk to ensure all foragers are in the hive and strap the hive to keep the equipment from moving. You can move your nuc in the dark or the next morning to the new location where it will be put in its permanent hive. Take off the strap and open the entrance to your nuc and watch your bees make their orientation flights. Moving a beehive is traumatic for bees so you need to leave them alone for 24 hours. Usually the frame of honey/beebread is gone and brood laid in the cells, so you will need to feed them. Follow the directions when placing a nuc into its permanent hive. After they are in their new home, it's a good idea to leave them alone for a few days. You may want to do like I do and just watch and listen to them as you sit next to the hive and talk to them.

From this point on, you can take care of your bees as you did the first year.

———————————

You should start to be familiar with the sounds of your hive after the second year of beekeeping. If you have developed a passion for bees and honor them, you may hear the hive's song in the third year. It could be sooner if you are gifted. I promise you, beekeeping is worth it. Each hive has a different song, and I have heard three of them. So will you! By the end of the third year, you will be confident enough that your bees will work with you. I can still remember the four bees that created a circle and backed a yellow jacket up to my thumb for me to squash it. For some beekeepers who honor their bees and develop a passion for them, the bees become their sisters – especially after they honor you by singing their hive's song.

Read all your books. Ask your questions. Go to your meetings. In the end, your bees will be your teachers.

11: Planting Your Garden

Planting your garden is one of the best gifts for your bees. If you watch your bees, you will learn that they don't care much for hybrids and prefer the wild or heirloom plants. When I first planted my herb garden over 30 years ago, I discovered that hybrids were only created to make a larger *product* or one to transport over long distances. Take the strawberry for an example. Wild strawberries have intense flavor over the domesticated varieties. The same goes for fragrance in flowers. The carnation is far less fragrant than the intensely aromatic dianthus family of flowers from which it was cultivated. Something is always lost when hybridizing any plant be it flowers, shrubs, fruits, or vegetables.

Plants Your Bees Like

Starting on the next page is a table of what plants my honeybees like in our agricultural 5/6 zone of the Appalachian Mountains in northwest North Carolina.[lxiii] It includes the plant type, its common and Latin names, bloom month, and source for honeybees. Google your zone for bee plants or check with your local agricultural office.

Trees & Shrubs

PLANT TYPE	COMMON NAME	LATIN NAME	BLOOM MONTH	SOURCE FOR HONEYBEES
F	Anise hyssop	*Agstache foeniculum*	7	minor
F	Blue Bugle Herb, Bugleweed, Carpetweed, Common bugle	*Ajuga reptans*	5	
F	Chives	*Allium schoenoprasum*	5	minor
C, F	Garlic Chives	*Allium tuberosa*	8	minor
F	Leadwort	*Amorpha fruticosa*	6	minor
F	Milkweed	*Asclepias* spp. 55 species	7	Major, 120-250 lbs. honey, soil dependent, good fertilization, *Asclepias syriaca* has the highest honey yield
F	Butterfly Weed	*Asclepias tuberosa*	7	minor
C	Asparagus	*Asparagus officinalis*	5	minor
F	Milk Vetch	*Astragalus* spp.	5	minor
F	Aster	*Aster* spp.	8	major[3]
F	Borage	*Borago officinalis*	6	minor, but can be major on cultivated area 200 lbs. honey per acre; 60-160 lbs. pollen
C, F	Mustard	*Brassica arvenisi (L.); Brassica campestris*	4	minor?

Trees & Shrubs

PLANT TYPE	COMMON NAME	LATIN NAME	BLOOM MONTH	SOURCE FOR HONEYBEES
C	Oilseed Rape (Canola)	*Brassica napus L., Brassica rapa*	5	major
F	Marigold	*Calendula officinalis*	6	minor
F	Canada Thistle	*Carduus arvensis*		
F	Thistle	*Centaurea* spp.	7	minor
F	Mountain Bluet	*Centaurea Montana* (Knapweed)	5	major
F	Creeping Thistle	*Cirsium arvense*	7	
F	Sweet Autumn Clematis	Clematis terniflora	9	minor
F	Clethra Summersweet	*Clethra alnifolia*	7	minor
C, F	Cucumber		6	minor
C	Melon		6	minor
C	Pumpkin	*Cucurbita pepo*	6	minor
C, F	Wild Carrot	*Daucus carota*	8	minor
F	Leopardsbane	*Doronicum cordatum*	4	minor
F	Candytuft	*Iberis sempervirens*	5	
F	Viper's Bugloss, Blue Thistle, Blue Weed	*Echium vulgare Echium vulgare* is most widely known, though there are about 60 additional species.	6	major 300-1,000 lbs. honey/acre depending on soil... 500-2,000 lbs of dark blue pollen.

139

Trees & Shrubs

PLANT TYPE	COMMON NAME	LATIN NAME	BLOOM MONTH	SOURCE FOR HONEYBEES
F	Globe Thistle	*Echinops ritro*	8	major
F	Fireweed	*Epilobium angustifolium*	6	major
F	Heather	*Erica vulgaris*, though many varieties		100-200 lbs. honey
F	Joe-Pye Weed, Boneset, White Snakeroot	*Eutrochium* spp. "*Eupatorium spp.* Eupatorium purpureum; Eupatorium perfoliatum; Eupatorium ageratoides	8	minor
C, F	Buckwheat	*Fagopyrum esculentum*	7	minor
F	Blue vine	*Gonolobus laevis*		minor, strong hives can collect up to 100 lbs.
C, F	Soybean	*Glycine soja*	7	major
C, F	Sunflower	*Helianthus annuus*	6	minor 30 - 100 pounds/acre
C, F	Basil	*Koellia*		minor
F	Henbit Deadnettle	*Lamium sp*	3	minor but valuable due to earliness/frost hardiness
C, F	Lavender	*Lavandula angustifolia*	6	minor
F	Birdsfoot Trefoil	*Lotus corniculatus*	6	minor
C, F	White Sweet Clover	*Melilotus alba*	5	major up to 200 pounds per hive

Trees & Shrubs

PLANT TYPE	COMMON NAME	LATIN NAME	BLOOM MONTH	SOURCE FOR HONEYBEES
C, F	Yellow Sweet Clover	*Melilotus officinalis*	5	major up to 200 lbs. per hive
C, F	Alfalfa	*Medicago sativa*	7	major
C, F	Clover	*Melilotus* spp. and *Trifolium* spp.	5	major, up to 500 pounds per acre in a good year
F	Melissa, Lemon Balm	*Melissa officinalis*		150-250 lbs. honey per acre; 50-120 lbs. pollen
C, F	Peppermint	*Mentha piperita*		
F	Catnip, Cat mint	*Nepeta mussinii*; *Nepeta grandiflora*; *Nepeta cataria*	6	minor
F	Oregano	*Origanum vulgare*	6	minor
C, F	Poppy	*Papaver somniferum*		minor, 20-30 pounds/acre
F	Russian Sage	*Perovskia atriplicifolia*	7	minor
C, F	Phacelia, Tansy	*Phacelia tanacetifolia*		180-1,500 lbs. honey per acre, depending on soil quality and depth; 300-1,000 lbs. of pollen.
G,H	Plantain	*Plantago Major*	7	
F	Smartweed	*Polygonum* spp.	8	major
F	Selfheal	*Prunella vulgaris*	7	minor
F	Lungwort	*Pulmonaria* spp.	5	minor

141

Trees & Shrubs

PLANT TYPE	COMMON NAME	LATIN NAME	BLOOM MONTH	SOURCE FOR HONEYBEES
F	Appalachian Mountain Mint	*Pycnanthemum flexuosum*	8	minor
F	Azalea	*Rhododendron* spp.	6	minor
F	Scrophularia	*Scrophularia* spp.	7	minor
F	Sedum, Autumn Joy	*Sedum spectabile*		
F	Goldenrod	*Solidago* spp.	9	major
F	Woundwort	*Stachys byzantina*	5	minor
F	Chickweed	*Stellaria Media*	4	minor
F	Dandelion	*Taraxacum officinale*	4	major
F	Germander, Thyme	*Teucrium canadense*	7	minor
F	Thyme	*Thymus pulegioides; Thymus serpyllum*	6	minor, 50-150 lbs. honey/acre
F	Red-Flowering Thyme	*Thymus praecox*	6	major
C, F	Alsike Clover	*Trifolium hybridum*		major, up to 500 pounds/acre
C, F	Crimson clover	*Trifolium incarnatum*		major
C, F	Red Clover	*Trifolium pratense*	6	major
C, F	White Clover	*Trifolium repens*	6	major
F	Blue Vervain	*Verbena hastata L.*	7	minor
F	Tall Ironweed	*Vernonia altissima*	8	minor

Trees & Shrubs

PLANT TYPE	COMMON NAME	LATIN NAME	BLOOM MONTH	SOURCE FOR HONEYBEES
F	Speedwell	*Veronica spicata*	6	minor
F	Tufted Vetch, Common Vetch[3]	*Vicia cracca*	7	minor
F	Common Vetch	*Vicia sativa*	7	minor
F	Blackhaw	*Viburnum prunifolium*	5	minor

It is best to ingest honey from within 10 miles of your residence, and no more than 50 miles because honey is very useful for plant allergies. The bees collect the vitamins and minerals from different sources and add more bee magic from their bodies to give humans one of the most healing, complex, and complete foods.

Common Foods, Herbs & Weeds

ITEM	VITAMIN / MINERAL	SEASON	USE/PURPOSE	VARROA
All Greens	Minerals	Spring/Fall	Whole Body	
Apple	Vitamin C	Summer/Fall	Immune System	
Apricot	Vitamin C	Summer/Fall	Immune System	
Alfalfa	Calcium	Summer	Skeletal Muscles Immune System	
Asparagus	Vitamin C	Spring/Summer	Immune System	
Basil	Calcium	Summer	Skeletal Muscles Immune System	
Bee Balm	Nectar	Summer		

Common Foods, Herbs & Weeds

ITEM	VITAMIN / MINERAL	SEASON	USE/PURPOSE	VARROA
Blueberry	Vitamin C	Summer	Immune System	
Beet, Sugar	Vitamin C	Summer/Biennial	Immune System	Oxalic Acid
Broccoli	Vitamin C	Summer	Immune System	
Brussels Sprouts	Vitamin C	Summer/Biennial	Immune System	
Burdock	Calcium	Summer	Skeletal Muscles Immune System	
Cabbage	Vitamin C	Summer/Biennial	Immune System	Oxalic Acid
Carrot	Vitamins A & C	Summer/Biennial	Immune System	
Catnip	Calcium	Summer	Skeletal Muscles Immune System	
Cauliflower	Vitamin C	Summer/Biennial	Immune System	
Cherry	Vitamin C	Spring/Summer	Immune System	
Chickweed	Calcium	Spring/Fall	Skeletal Muscles Immune System	
Chives	Vitamins B & C	Summer	Immune System	Oxalic Acid
Chokecherry	Vitamin C	Summer	Immune System	
Comfrey Leaf	Calcium	Summer/Fall	Skeletal Muscles Immune System	
Crabapple	Vitamin C	Spring	Immune System	
Cranberry	Vitamin C	Spring	Immune System	
Dandelion	Nectar	Spring	Liver Toner	

Common Foods, Herbs & Weeds

ITEM	VITAMIN / MINERAL	SEASON	USE/PURPOSE	VARROA
Dill Weed	Calcium	Summer	Skeletal Muscles Immune System	
Eggplant	Vitamin C	Spring	Immune System	
Elderberry		Spring/Summer	Immune System	
Fireweed	Nectar	Summer		
Garlic	Vitamin C	Spring	Immune System	
Grape	Vitamin C	Spring/Summer	Immune System	
Hawk's Beard	Nectar	Summer		
Kale	Vitamin C & Calcium	Spring/Fall	Immune System	
Kiwi Fruit	Vitamin C	Spring	Immune System	
Lettuce	Vitamin C	Spring/Fall	Immune System	
Licorice	Calcium	Spring/Fall	Skeletal Muscles Immune System	
Loganberry	Vitamin C	Spring	Immune System	
Marjoram	Calcium	Summer	Skeletal Muscles Immune System	
Marshmallow	Calcium	Summer/Fall	Skeletal Muscles Immune System	
Melons	Vitamin C	Spring/Summer	Immune System	
Mints	Calcium	Summer/Fall	Skeletal Muscles Immune System	Menthol
Nettle	Calcium	Fall	Skeletal Muscles Immune System	Formic Acid

Common Foods, Herbs & Weeds

ITEM	VITAMIN / MINERAL	SEASON	USE/PURPOSE	VARROA
Oregano	Calcium	Summer	Skeletal Muscles Immune System	
Parsley	Vitamin C	Summer	Immune System	Oxalic Acid
Pawpaw	Vitamin C	Spring	Immune System	
Peach	Vitamin C	Spring	Immune System	
Pear	Vitamin C	Spring	Immune System	
Pepper, Red or Green Chili	Vitamin C	Summer	Immune System	
Pepper, Red	Vitamin C	Spring	Immune System	
Peppermint	Calcium	Summer/Fall	Skeletal Muscles Immune System	Menthol
Peas	Vitamin B & Minerals	Spring/Fall		Oxalic Acid
Potatoes	Vitamin B & Minerals	Spring/Fall	Immune System	Oxalic Acid
Purslane				Oxalic Acid
Raspberry	Vitamin C	Spring	Immune System	
Red Clover	Calcium	Summer	Skeletal Muscles Immune System	Oxalic Acid
Red Currant	Vitamin C	Spring	Immune System	
Red Raspberry	Calcium	Summer	Skeletal Muscles Immune System	
Rhubarb	Vitamins C & K & Minerals	Spring		Oxalic Acid

Common Foods, Herbs & Weeds

ITEM	VITAMIN / MINERAL	SEASON	USE/PURPOSE	VARROA
Rose Hip	Vitamin C	Summer	Immune System	
Rosemary (mint family)	Calcium	Summer/Fall	Skeletal Muscles Immune System	
Sage	Calcium	Spring/Summer	Skeletal Muscles Immune System	
Savory	Calcium	Spring		
Skullcap	Calcium	Summer	Skeletal Muscles Immune System	
Spinach	Vitamin C	Spring/Fall	Immune System	
Strawberry	Vitamin C	Spring/Summer	Immune System	
Thymus Serpyllum	Calcium	Summer	Skeletal Muscles Immune System	Thymol
Tomato	Vitamin C	Spring/Summer	Immune System	
Vitex		Summer	Female Hormone Balance	
Watermelon	Vitamin C	Spring	Immune System	
Willow	Nectar	Spring	Skeletal Muscles Immune System	
Wolfberry (Goji)	Vitamin C	Summer		

In the above list under Varroa, you will notice that the natural acids and oils the commercial beekeepers use in the hive are also in the plants listed. Actually, they are in most of the plants that the bees harvest. It is best to let the bee put the acids into the honey that is fed to the larvae rather than putting it inside the hive. The bees know how much they need of anything.

Chemicals Hazardous to Honeybees

Earlier, we talked about how dangerous glyphosate is. You should also know about some other chemicals that are hazardous to honeybees when fertilizing your trees, shrubs, and other plants. The below list is not a complete list, but it provides you with the most common chemicals used today.

VERY HAZARDOUS	MODERATELY HAZARDOUS
Azinphosmethyul Benzene Hexachloride Carbaryl Chlorphyriphos Crotanomide Diazinon Fenthion Heptachlor Lindane Malathion Methyl Parathion Methomyl Monocrotophos Parathion Propoxur	Chlordane Demeton Endosulfan Endrin Oxamyl Phorate

In recent years, there is a growing concern of what the combination of chemicals in honey, wax, propolis, and more may do when consumed by pollinators and humans. We are already seeing the devastations done with Neonics and glyphosate in Roundup® working together synergistically. When purchasing your plants, ask what chemicals were used.

12: Fascinating Facts

The Charged Flower

Scientists have known about the electric side of pollination since the 1960s. As bees fly through the air, they bump into charged particles from dust to small molecules. The friction of these microscopic collisions strips electrons from the bee's surface, and they typically end up with a positive charge. However, flowers tend to have a negative charge – at least on clear days. The flowers themselves are electrically charged, but the air around them carries a voltage of around 100 volts for every meter above the ground. The positive charge that accumulates around the flower induces a negative charge in its petals.[lxiv]

When the positively charged bee arrives at the negatively charged flower, sparks don't fly but pollen does. The bee may fly over to the flower but at close quarters, the flower also flies to the bee.[lxv] This charge also indicates when there is nectar in the flower. Ninety seconds after the last nectar has been taken from the flower, the flower will no longer emit a static charge.

Bees See Heat Patterns in Flowers

The heat patterns in the flowers look the same to humans. However, bumblebees, honeybees, and stingless bees use thermal detectors in their antennae and tarsi to help figure out which flowers are which.[lxvi] See how bees see heat patterns in flowers in the picture above.

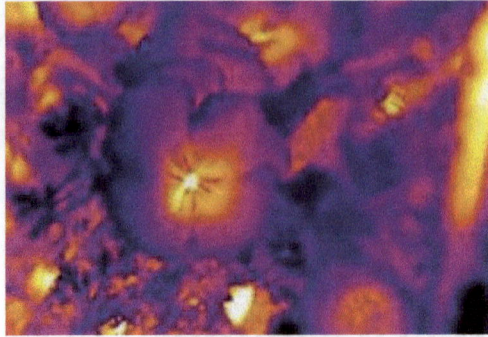

Bumblebees, who visit a wide range of different flowers, were found using these patterns to distinguish between different flowers and the rewards that they provide. Not only are the pattern differences good for efficient foraging, the heat from the flower warms the pollinator.

Who Decides the Caste

Everyone thinks the queen decides if she lays worker or drone eggs. Actually, it is the workers that decide what the colony needs. They build the cell part way up in preparation for the egg. The diameter indicates what caste they want the queen to lay. The queen examines the cell to be sure the cell is clean and has a dollop of royal jelly in the bottom. She then spreads her back legs across the cell. If the cell is large, she will lay a drone egg. If the cell is smaller, she will lay a worker egg.

Bees Can Smell

Honeybees have 170 odorant-receptor genes. This is twice what Drosophila (fruit flies) and Anopheles (mosquitos) have.[lxvii] I am a diabetic, and my bees don't seem to mind my breath as it is sweet smelling. It is totally different if I eat anything stronger than my sweet breath.

Humans also emit pheromones. When they are afraid, they will emit the fear pheromone. Like dogs that will bite when they smell fear, bees will sting when they smell the fear pheromone. I have found that when I enter my apiary with a man, the man will get stung and I will not because of the difference between male and female hormones. I have been told by other women that when they enter the yard while they are in their monthly cycle, the bees seem to treat them with more kindness or as one beekeeper told me, "with a whole lot of loving."

Bee Venom and Hormones

On the BEe Healing Guild.Org website, there is a blog about Human Hormones.[lxviii] I briefed here because it is vital that you understand the affects bee venom has on the human body and why it can be contraindicating.

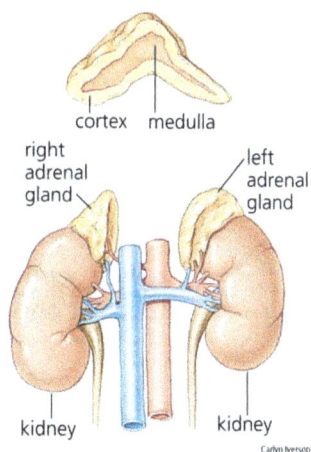

cortex medulla

right adrenal gland

left adrenal gland

kidney   kidney

Carlyn Iverson

Adrenal Cortex Hormones:

When the body is under stress (pain) due to bee stings, the hypothalamus is alerted and releases corticotrophin-releasing hormone (CRH) that stimulates the pituitary gland to release adrenal corticotropic hormone (ACTH) from the adrenal glands.

Both the Adrenal Cortex Hormones and Adrenal Medulla Hormones alert the adrenal glands to produce corticosteroid hormones from the adrenal cortex; one of which are the

151

androgens that are also produced in testes and ovaries. Part of the problem for women diagnosed with Polycystic Ovary Syndrome is that **PCOS** produces androgens, causes insulin resistance, high testosterone, diabetes, weight gain, difficult cycles, and more. Cortisol lingers in the body and accumulates, contributing to diseases such as obesity, diabetes, heart disease, and cancer. The cortisol released after a bee sting increases the effects of PCOS.

Adrenal Medulla Hormones

At the same time the stress of bee stings causes the adrenal cortex to respond, the sympathetic nervous system is stimulated and neurotransmitters cause flight/fight response. The medulla produces catecholamines: adrenaline, noradrenaline, and a little dopamine. The hormones released by the medulla are:

- Epinephrine (also known as adrenaline) responds by increasing your pulse and pushing blood to muscles and the brain. It also spikes your blood sugar. **DIABETES.**
- Norepinephrine (also known as noradrenaline) is made in the brain and the nervous system. It works with epinephrine.

If norepinephrine is too low, it can lead to **DEPRESSION** and **ADHD**, or too high contributes to anxiety. If someone on anti-depression medication also receives bee stings, they will experience blisters or rash on the skin due to too much norepinephrine. Because there are so many hormones in the brain that are generated by the body, it is very difficult to treat for depression. Both hormones can cause a person receiving a bee sting to experience a "high" or euphoric sensation and will last only a short moment.

Both hormones are also associated with **PTSD** which from personal experience can radically affect your short-term memory. Because these hormones are released during stress, they may cause you to forget your answers when you are taking an important test. If you relax and deeply breathe through the anxiety, all will be fine. So, sometimes bee stings may cause a temporary memory loss.

Afterword

The message I want most to convey in this book is that, at all times, you honor the hive as though it is your hive/home, and you honor the honeybees as though they are your children. They are your children while they are in your care, but you also need to remember that they belong to Mother and you should nurture and tend to Her children as She would.

The honeybee can communicate with you and to you on levels you may not have explored. Being mindful while in the apiary focused only on your bees will help you to open up your senses. Listening to the different levels of the sounds of the buzzing will indicate what is going on in the hive. Watching their movements in their waggle dancing or being scattered when the hive is opened is another way of letting you know what is happening. Smelling the warm honey at different times of the year will tell you what is being harvested or if something is wrong in the hive. Even touching their wings can give you a tiny electrical current.

I always suggest that, if possible, students (newbies) get a mentor and attend bee meetings so that they can gain all the knowledge available to be a better beekeeper. They don't have to agree with others, but the newbie should listen and communicate with humans as well. As a treatment-free beekeeper, I have been verbally and actually physically abused. So, I suggest to the newbie to not share the idea that they are treatment-free and to just listen. Perhaps you as the newbie can share your knowledge with those who do treat, but this can only happen after three years of no treatments.

The honeybee's intelligence is higher than other pollinators. Solitary bees of 10,000 years ago have evolved into colonies that behave and work together as superorganisms that can sense and regulate hive temperature, and much more. Even though hive tasks are usually based on the age of the bee, the bee can change their roles as needed. They can count to three, see colors, know basic symbols, and can be trained to a small degree. The honeybee is the most profound animal because it is responsible for one-third of our food and is the most important pollinator because it maintains the integrity of our food by not cross pollinating.

The honeybees' nutritional needs are similar to humans. They need to feed on organically or naturally grown plants that have not been sprayed with any -*cides*. The more organic the beehive products are, the more healing the hive products will be. The honeybee is the only animal I know that holds the key to healing over 500 modern diseases using their hive products, including their larvae. They harvest resin to make propolis to heal cancer, MRSA, tumors, and much more. Nectar's water is dried out to about 18% to make honey that can heal open wounds like no modern medicine can. Honey can sustain a person for six months. The only reason they cannot go longer is that it doesn't contain enough protein to sustain muscles. The bee's add honey to the pollen, and the enzymes and lactic acid in the honey break down the pollen's tough outer shell. After the shell is opened, the pollen is fermented into beebread and is the bee's protein used to make muscles. Pollen is also needed by the bees to make royal jelly and bee venom. The bees obtain their vitamins/minerals from nature and put those properties and some of their own magic into each and every hive product. The bees add hydrogen peroxide to the honey, making it another reason honey doesn't go bad and helps in healing wounds.

156

Using bee products to heal is called Apitherapy, the world in which I spiritually learned about honeybees. On a spiritual level, the honeybee can teach you to listen to your environment, as well as show you how to reach within yourself and find your own antennae. Using your inner senses can open you up and allow you to reach a portal into a soul. What happens from that point can be a life-altering experience.

Honeybee can sense a flower's heat patterns, and receive an electrical current from a flower containing nectar. You also read in this book how honeybees need the electrical energy of 190-250 hertz to get rid of pests. I have continually heard and read that bees need water to cool the hive. But I have another theory. In order for water to carry electricity, it needs to contain some impurities to magnify the electrical current as are in the earth's geomagnetic lines. I often wondered if the honeybee bring water into the hive and spread the moisture with their wings, adding more impurities from the air, in order to bring the electrical hertz up to 190-250. This way, the hive would always carry the current throughout the hive even when it isn't placed over the geomagnetic lines. It would be a fascinating study.

References

i Stabentheiner, A., Kovac, H., Brodschneider, R. (2010, January 2). Honeybee Colony Thermoregulation – Regulatory Mechanisms and Contribution of Individuals in Dependence on Age, Location and Thermal Stress. *PLOS One, 5(1),* e8967. Doi: doi.org/10.1371/journal.pone.0008967.
http://journals.plos.org/plosone/article?id=10.1371/journal.pone.0008967.

ii Steiner, Rudolf. (1907, September 14). Occult Signs and Symbols.
http://wn.rsarchive.org/Lectures/GA101/English/AP1972/19070914p01.html.

iii Lorenzen, I. (1938). *The Spiritual Foundations of Beekeeping.* Hamburg, Germany: Schultz & Thiele.

iv Haarmann, T., Spivak, M., Weaver, D., et al. (2002, February 9). Effects of Fluvalinate and Coumaphos on Queen Honey Bees (Hymenoptera: Apidae) in Two Commercial Queen Rearing Operations. *Journal of Economic Entomology, 95(1),* 28-35. https://www.ncbi.nlm.nih.gov/pubmed/11942761.

v Tan, K., Yang, S., Wang, Z., et. al. (2013, June 13). Effect of Flumethrin on Survival and Olfactory Learning in Honeybees. *PLoS ONE 8(6),* e66295.
http://journals.plos.org/plosone/article?id=10.1371/journal.pone.0066295.

vi https://en.wikipedia.org/wiki/Varroa_jacobsoni

vii Seeley, T. D., D. R. Tarpy, S. R. Griffin, A. Carcione, and D. A. Delaney. 2015. A survivor population of wild colonies of European honeybees in the northeastern United States: investigating its genetic structure. Apidologie 46:654–666.

viii Ins. Sec. Life 2: 109-114, 1998. Observation on apis Mellifera Ligustuca spin. Hived on Foundation with Different Cell Base Size. M. Accorsi M., De Pace F., Lute F., Baggio A., Baracani G., Massi S., Sabatini AG, Sommaruga A., Observation on Apis mellifera ligustica Spin, etc. Needs to be obtained from Cra Api Secretary.

ix http://beekeeperlinda.blogspot.com/2006/05/housel-positioning-for-honey-super.html

x Schwartz, L. (2016, March 22). Toxic Traps: When These 7 Types of Plastic are Dangerous. *ALTERNET online.* http://www.alternet.org/personal-health/toxic-traps-when-these-7-types-plastic-are-dangerous.

xi Types of Plastics. (n.d.). In *Grainger Safety: QuickTips Technical Resources online.* https://www.grainger.com/content/qt-types-of-plastics-213.

xii Covington, W. (1963, May 7). Frame and Plastic Comb Foundation for Beehives. *IFI CLAIMS Patent Services online.* https://www.google.com/patents/US3088135.

xiii Plastic Water Bottles Exposed to Heat Can be Toxic. (n.d.) *DRGEO online.* http://drgeo.com/plastic-water-bottlewws-exposed-to-heat-can-be-toxic/.

xiv Barry, C. (2009, August 20). Plastic Breaks Down in Ocean, After All – And Fast. *National Geographic News online.* http://news.nationalgeographic.com/news/2009/08/090820-plastic-decomposes-oceans-seas.html.

xv The Lowly Wax Worm May Hold the Key to Biodegrading Plastic. (2017, April 25). In *National Public Radio online.* https://www.npr.org/sections/thetwo-way/2017/04/25/525447206/a-worm-may-hold-the-key-to-biodegrading-plastic.

xvi Ley Lines. (n.d.) In *Wikipedia online.* https://en.wikipedia.org/wiki/Ley_line

xvii https://modernsurvivalblog.com/natural-disasters/the-honeybee-varroa-vibration-and-ccd/

xviii Schumann Resonance. (n.d.). In *National Aeronautics and Space Administration online.* https://www.nasa.gov/mission_pages/sunearth/news/gallery/schumann-resonance.html.

xix PowerToThePeople. (2017, January 18). Resonant Frequency is the Key. In *Minds online.* https://www.minds.com/blog/view/668610149551710221.

xx Schumann Resonances. (n.d.). In *Wikipedia online.* https://en.wikipedia.org/wiki/Schumann_resonances.

xxi Cell Size. (n.d.). *Resistantbees online.* http://www.resistantbees.com/zelle_e.html.

xxii http://beverlyblanchard.blogspot.com/2013/04/the-law-of-duality.html

xxiii Wenfu Mao, Mary A. Schuler, and May R. Berenbaum. 2015. A dietary phytochemical alters caste-associated gene expression in honey bees. Science Advances 1(7).

xxiv https://www.youtube.com/watch?v=N72KFpvIiss

xxv Zimmer, C. (2013, July 11). Unraveling the Pollinating Secrets of a Bee's Buzz. In *The New York Times online.* http://www.nytimes.com/2013/07/11/science/unraveling-the-pollinating-secrets-of-a-bees-buzz.html?_r=0.

xxvi Williams, Mark. (n.d.). Beekeeping with a Smoker. In *PerfectBee.* https://www.perfectbee.com/your-beehive/equipment-and-clothing/beekeeping-and-use-of-smokers/.

xxvii https://www.irishbeekeepersassociation.com/an-introduction-to-the-honey-bee.html

xxviii Wang, Y., Ma, L., Zhang, W., et al. (2015, July 4). Comparison of the Nutrient Composition of Royal Jelly and Worker Jelly of Honey Bees (*Apis mellifera).* *Apidologie, 47(1),* 48-56. https://link.springer.com/article/10.1007/s13592-015-0374-x.

[xxix] Journal of Chemical Ecology, Vol. 15, No. 6, 1989 Alarm Pheromone Production By Two Honeybee (Apis Mellifera) Types Anita M. Collins, 1 Thomas E. Rinderer, 1 Howell V. Daly, 2 John R. Harbo, 1 And Daniel Pesante 1
https://link.springer.com/article/10.1007/BF01012262

[xxx] Naturwissenschaften, July 1990, Volume 77, Issue 7, pp 334–336| Y. Le Conte, G. Arnold, J. Trouiller, C. Masson, B. Chappe
https://link.springer.com/article/10.1007%2FBF01138390

[xxxi] Odor-evoked responses to queen pheromone components and to plant odors using optical imaging in the antennal lobe of the honey bee drone *Apis mellifera* L. Jean-Christophe Sandoz. Journal of Experimental Biology 2006 209: 3587-3598; doi: 10.1242/jeb.02423 http://jeb.biologists.org/content/209/18/3587.full

[xxxii] Behavioral Ecology and Sociobiology, July 2005, Volume 58, Issue 3, pp 270–276| Dufour's gland pheromone as a reliable fertility signal among honeybee (*Apis mellifera*) workers. Roi Dor, Tamar Katzav-Gozansky, Abraham Hefetz
https://link.springer.com/article/10.1007/s00265-005-0923-9

[xxxiii] Journal of Chemical Ecolog. March 1981, Volume 7, Issue 2, pp 225–237|, The Nasonov pheromone of the honeybee *Apis mellifera* L. (Hymenoptera, Apidae). Part II. Bioassay of the components using foragers. Ingrid H. Williams, J. A. Pickett, A. P. Martin https://link.springer.com/article/10.1007/BF00995745

[xxxiv] Journal of Insect Behavior, September 1991, Volume 4, Issue 5, pp 649–660|, The role of queen mandibular pheromone and colony congestion in honey bee (*Apis mellifera* L.) reproductive swarming (Hymenoptera: Apidae), Mark L. Winston, Heather A. Higo, Simon J. Colley, Tanya Pankiw, Keith N. Slessor
https://link.springer.com/article/10.1007/BF01048076

[xxxv] Behavioral Ecology and Sociobiology, December 2005, Volume 59, Issue 2, pp 278–284| Retinue attraction and ovary activation: responses of wild type and anarchistic honey bees (*Apis mellifera*) to queen and brood pheromones, Shelley E. R. Hoover, Mark L. Winston, Benjamin P. Oldroyd.
https://link.springer.com/article/10.1007/s00265-005-0039-2

[xxxvi] Journal of Invertebrate Pathology. Volume 102, Issue 2, October 2009, Pages 91-96. Bacteria in the gut of Japanese honeybee, *Apis cerana japonica*, and their antagonistic effect against *Paenibacillus larvae*, the causal agent of American foulbrood, Mikio Yoshiyama, Kiyoshi Kimura.
https://doi.org/10.1016/j.jip.2009.07.005

[xxxvii] http://peacebeefarm.blogspot.com/2011/03/chilled-brood.html

[xxxviii] Lactobacillus apis sp. nov., from the stomach of honeybees (Apis mellifera), having an in vitro inhibitory effect on the causative agents of American and European foulbrood J. Killer,1,2 S. Dubna´, 3 I. Sedla´cˇek4 and P. Sˇ vec4. International Journal of Systematic and Evolutionary Microbiology (2014), 64, 152–157. DOI 10.1099/ijs.0.053033-0.

http://www.microbiologyresearch.org/docserver/fulltext/ijsem/64/1/152_ijs0530
33.pdf?expires=1531243634&id=id&accname=guest&checksum=1A681F10DDF0C
36A7BDD73F424D352B8

xxxix Proc Natl Acad Sci U S A. 2017 Mar 7; 114(10): 2538–2543., Published online
2017 Feb 13. doi: [10.1073/pnas.1614864114], PMCID: PMC5347564, PMID:
28193870. Disruption of quercetin metabolism by fungicide affects energy
production in honey bees (*Apis mellifera*), Wenfu Mao, Mary A. Schuler, and May R.
Berenbaum https://www.ncbi.nlm.nih.gov/pmc/articles/PMC5347564/

xl Anaerobe, Volume 20, April 2013, Pages 74-78. Pathogenesis and toxins,
Glyphosate suppresses the antagonistic effect of *Enterococcus*spp. on *Clostridium
botulinum*. Monika Krüger, Awad Ali Shehata, , Arne Rodloff
https://doi.org/10.1016/j.anaerobe.2013.01.005

xli http://www.entomology.wisc.edu/mbcn/fea207.html

xlii https://www.pnas.org/content/pnas/113/34/9486.full.pdf

xliii http://www.honeybeezen.com/worlds-supplier-nosema-medication-fumagilin-
b-shuts/

xliv Fallon, J., Reeves, E., Kavanagh, K. (2010, June). Inhibition of Neutrophil Function
Following Exposure to the Aspergillus Fumigatus Toxin Fumagillin. *Journal of
Medical Microbiology, 59(6)*, 625-633. Doi: 10.1099/jmm.0.01892-0.
https://www.ncbi.nlm.nih.gov/pubmed/20203215.

xlv Van den Heever, J. Thompson, T., Curtis, J., et al. (2014). Fumagillin: An Overview
of Recent Scientific Advances and Their Significance in Apiculture. *Journal of
Agriculture and Food Chemistry, 62(13)*, 2728-2737. Doi: 10.1021/jf4055374.
https://pubs.acs.org/doi/abs/10.1021/jf4055374?src=recsys&journalCode=jafcau.

xlvi Topolska, G. (2001). [Varroa Destructor (Anderson and Trueman, 2000); the
Change in Classification within the Genus Varroa (Oudemans, 1904)]. *Wiadmosci
Parazytologiczne, 47(1)*, 151-155.
https://www.ncbi.nlm.nih.gov/pubmed/16888966.

xlvii Extension. Honey Bee Viruses, the Deadly Varroa Mite Associates, Department of
Entomology and Plant Pathology, the University of Tennessee, Knoxville TN, August
21, 2014, Authors: Philip A. Moore, Michael E. Wilson, and John A. Skinner.
https://articles.extension.org/pages/71172/honey-bee-viruses-the-deadly-varroa-
mite-associates

xlviii Israeli Acute Paralysis Virus: Epidemiology, Pathogenesis and Implications for
Honey Bee Health, Published: July 31, 2014, Yan Ping Chen, Jeffery S. Pettis, Miguel
Corona, Wei Ping Chen, Cong Jun Li, Marla Spivak, P. Kirk Visscher, Gloria DeGrandi-
Hoffman, Humberto Boncristiani, Yan Zhao, Dennis vanEngelsdorp, Keith Delaplane,
Leellen Solter,, Jay D. Evans https://doi.org/10.1371/journal.ppat.1004261,

xlix https://en.wikipedia.org/wiki/Neonicotinoid

l Elsevier. The neonicotinoids thiacloprid, imidacloprid, and clothianidin affect the
immunocompetence of honey bees (Apis mellifera L.) Annely Brandt, Anna Gorenflo,

Reinhold Siede, Marina Meixner, Ralph Büchler LLH Bee Institute, Erlenstr. 9, 35274 Kirchhain, Germany. Journal of Insect Physiology 86 (2016) 40–47. Journal of Insect Physiology. https://boerenlandvogels.nl/sites/default/files/2017-12/Annely%20Brandt%20et%20al%202016.pdf

[li] Ptaszynska, A., Borsuk, G., Zdybicka-Barabas, A., et. al. (2015, October 6). Are Commercial and Prebiotics Effective in the Treatment and Prevention of Honeybee Nosemosis C? *Parasitology Research, 115,* 397-406. Doi: 10.1007/s00436-015-4761-z. http://www.ncbi.nlm.nih.gov/pmc/articles/PMC4700093/.

[lii] Vojodic, S., Rehan, S & Anderson, K. (2013, August 21). Microbial Gut Diversity of Africanized and European Honey Bee Larval Instars. *PLoS ONE, 8(8),* e72106. Doi: 10.1371/journal.pone.0072106. http://journals.plos.org/plosone/article?id=10.1371%2Fjournal.pone.0072106.

[liii] Hutkins, R. & Nannen, N. (1993, September). pH Homeostasis in Lactic Acid Bacteria. *University of Nebraska – Lincoln, Food Science and Technology Department.* http://digitalcommons.unl.edu/cgi/viewcontent.cgi?article=1028&context=foodsciefacpub.

[liv] Vojodic, S., Rehan, S & Anderson, K. (2013, August 21). Microbial Gut Diversity of Africanized and European Honey Bee Larval Instars. *PLoS ONE, 8(8),* e72106. Doi: 10.1371/journal.pone.0072106. http://journals.plos.org/plosone/article?id=10.1371%2Fjournal.pone.0072106.

[lv] Toporcak, J., Nemcova, R., Gancarcikova, S., et. al. (2011, September 19). Lactobacillus sp. as a Potential Probiotic for the Prevention of Paenibacillus Larvae Infection in Honey Bees. *Journal of Apitcultural Research, 50(4),* 323-324. Doi abs.10.3896.IBRA.1.50.4.11.http://www.tandfonline.com/doi/abs/10.3896/IBRA.1.50.4.11.

[lvi] Ingham, C., Beerthuyzen, M. & Vlieg, J. (2008, December). Population Heterogeneity of Lactobacillus Plantarum WCFS1 Microcolonies in Response to and Recovery from Acid Stress. *Applied and Environmental Microbiology,* 7750-7758. Doi: 10.1128/AEM.00982-08. http://aem.asm.org/content/74/24/7750.full.pdf+html.

[lvii] Evan, J. & Lopez, D. (2004, July). Bacterial Probiotics Induce an Immune Response in Honey Bee (Hymenoptera: Apidae). *Journal of Economic Entomology, 97(3),* 752-756. https://www.researchgate.net/publication/8431169_Bacterial_Probiotics_Induce_an_Immune_Response_in_the_Honey_Bee_Hymenoptera_Apidae.

[lviii] Ptaszynska, A., Borsuk, G., Zdybicka-Barabas, A., et. al. (2015, October 6). Are Commercial and Prebiotics Effective in the Treatment and Prevention of Honeybee Nosemosis C? *Parasitology Research, 115,* 397-406. Doi: 10.1007/s00436-015-4761-z. http://www.ncbi.nlm.nih.gov/pmc/articles/PMC4700093/.

[lix] https://www.thehealthyhomeeconomist.com/make-raw-apple-cider-vinegar/

[lx] https://supremevinegar.com/2016/08/22/white-distilled-vinegar-ingredients-explained/

163

[lxi] Metabolism of Fructophilic Lactic Acid Bacteria Isolated from the *Apis mellifera* L. Bee Gut: Phenolic Acids as External Electron Acceptors. Appl Environ Microbiol. 2016 Dec 1; 82(23): 6899–6911. Pasquale Filannino, Raffaella Di Cagno,⬚ Rocco Addante, Erica Pontonio, and Marco Gobbetti.
https://www.ncbi.nlm.nih.gov/pmc/articles/PMC5103089/

[lxii] https://en.wikipedia.org/wiki/Buckfast_bee

[lxiii] List of Northern American Nectar Sources for Honey Bees. (n.d.). In *Wikipedia online.*
https://en.wikipedia.org/wiki/Northern_American_nectar_sources_for_honey_bees.

[lxiv] Honey Bees Electrically "Shock Charge" Flowers. (2013, March 19). In *beeu online.*
https://beeuorganics.wordpress.com/2013/03/19/honey-bees-electrically-shock-charge-flowers/.

[lxv] Yong, E. (2013, February 21). Bees Can Sense the Electric Fields of Flowers. In *National Geographic online.*
http://phenomena.nationalgeographic.com/2013/02/21/bees-can-sense-the-electric-fields-of-flowers/.

[lxvi] Breyer, M. (2017, December 20). Flowers Use Secret Language to Lure Bees. In *treehugger online.* https://www.treehugger.com/natural-sciences/flowers-use-secret-language-lure-bees.html.

[lxvii] Sandoz, J., Deisig, N., de Brito Sanchez., et. al. (2007, February). Understanding the Logics of Pheromone Processing in the Honeybee Brain: From Labeled-Lines to Across-Fiber Patterns. *Frontiers in Behavioral Neuroscience, 1(5)*, 1-12. Doi: 10.3389/neuro.08.005.2007.
https://www.researchgate.net/profile/Martin_Giurfa/publication/23425876_Understanding_the_Logics_of_Pheromone_Processing_in_the_Honeybee_Brain_From_Labeled-Lines_to_Across-Fiber_Patterns/links/00463521d058aa94a3000000/Understanding-the-Logics-of-Pheromone-Processing-in-the-Honeybee-Brain-From-Labeled-Lines-to-Across-Fiber-Patterns.pdf.

[lxviii] https://www.endocrineweb.com/endocrinology/overview-adrenal-glands

www.ingramcontent.com/pod-product-compliance
Lightning Source LLC
Chambersburg PA
CBHW060041030426
42334CB00019B/2427